Stories That Live

Stories That Live

Edited or written by **Ralph V. Cutlip**
Formerly Chairman, English Department
San Gabriel High School
San Gabriel, California

Dedicated to serving

our nation's youth

When ordering this book, you may specify:
either **R 137 P** *or* **Stories That Live**

AMSCO SCHOOL PUBLICATIONS, INC.
315 Hudson Street New York, N. Y. 10013

Acknowledgments

Grateful acknowledgment is made to the following sources for permission to reprint copyrighted stories or for other courtesies. The stories begin in this book on the pages indicated.

Doubleday & Company, Inc. *Page 24.* "Jimmy Valentine" adapted from "A Retrieved Reformation." From *Road to Destiny* by O. Henry. Reprinted by permission of Doubleday & Company, Inc. *Page 101.* "The Ransom of Red Chief" from *Whirligigs* by O. Henry. Copyright 1907 by Doubleday & Company, Inc. Reprinted by permission of the publisher.

Lois Duncan, *Page 134.* "Written in the Stars," copyright © 1959 by Lois Duncan. Appeared originally in *Seventeen.* Adapted by permission of the author and McIntosh and Otis, Inc.

Random House, Inc. *Page 13.* "God Sees the Truth but Waits" by Leo Tolstoy. *Page 77.* "The Servant" by S. T. Semonov. Both stories adapted and reprinted from *Best Russian Short Stories* by courtesy of Random House, Inc.

Irving Shepard. *Page 88.* "Love of Life," copyright by Irving Shepard.

Illustrated by Harry Kane

Printed in the United States of America

To the Student

Do you like to watch exciting adventure tales on TV or on the movie screen? If you do, you will like the stories in this book.

Did you know that reading a story can be more fun than watching one on a film? Why is this true? When you see a filmed story, your attention is under pressure to keep up with the fast-moving plot. You are a prisoner of the whirl-wind action of the mechanical devices that bring you the pictures and the sound. You do not have much opportunity to think about the story. You do not have enough time to draw the full enjoyment from the adventure and live it in your imagination as you would like to.

On the other hand, when you read a story, you have time to think about the characters, and you get a better understanding of why they act the way they do. You have a better opportunity to think about the plot. There is a greater challenge to your intelligence.

When you saw the title of this book, you might have asked: "What makes a story live?"

Stories live only when they appeal to our sense of what is real, that is, when they seem true to life. Stories live only when they are written in an interesting way. Stories live only when they satisfy our desire for adventure.

Perhaps you have said to yourself at one time or another, "I don't like to read" or "Reading takes too much time." It is quite possible that some of the things you tried to read were not interesting, were too difficult, or did not appeal to your imagination.

The stories in this book have been selected on the basis of their interest for young people. The stories include a variety of subjects—mystery, humor, adventure, sports, romance, the sea, and military life.

You will like the stories for the following reasons:

1. The stories are related to life.
2. Each story tells about a dramatic incident.
3. The stories will appeal to your imagination and to your intelligence.
4. The stories are written clearly and are not difficult to read.

You have some exciting moments ahead of you. Enjoy yourself!

Ralph V. Cutlip

Contents

CONTENTS

Andy and the
One-Inch Rope

Ralph V. Cutlip

I

Andy Todd smiled in satisfaction as his earth-drilling machine hummed steadily with mighty power. His digger had already reached a depth of ten feet in the hole he was boring. It was one of over a hundred the road department was digging to be filled with concrete to strengthen the base of a hill below a street-widening project. The holes he had dug ranged in depth from twelve to fifteen feet and were slightly more than sixteen inches in diameter.

Andy was black, slender, and clean-faced. His teeth shone brightly through his broad smile. He lived at home with his mother and little sister. He was the sole[1] support of the family although his mother earned a small amount of money at house-

(*Note:* The numbered words or expressions in each of these stories are explained in "Building Your Vocabulary" at the end of the story.)

1

cleaning in different neighborhoods during the afternoons. She hoped and dreamed that Andy would go to college some day. "You kin make it, boy," she had said a thousand times. "Just you mind yore own bizness and pay no mind to rascals who try to git you in trouble—makes no never mind if they's white or black!"

The machine responded easily and quickly to the control levers, as Andy's long arms moved them back and forth. The front end had a set of crablike claws that held the long drill stem in place. The machine shook and rocked when he raised the drill or lowered it into the hole.

Other machines clanked and roared on the construction project. A road scraper crawled along the roadway; and an earthmover bumped along, its belly filled with earth and rocks. A clamshell digger[2] dug a deep hole for a bridge foundation.

It was Andy's first week as a machine operator, and he felt happy in a new kind of work. He had laughingly spoken of his previous job as that of a "pick-and-shovel artist." But Andy hadn't minded all the hard work. He knew he had to start somewhere.

He had had a busy morning; and when he looked at the long line of stakes that traced the foot of the hill, he realized there was much work to do. Then he began to wonder what had delayed the cement truck. There were still three holes to be filled and it was now almost noon.

He was suddenly aware that the other workers had left their stations and were moving into the shade of a tree to eat lunch. He turned off the engine, laid his hard hat on the seat, and climbed down from the machine cab. Going to his buddy's car, he got his own lunchpail and joined the group in the shade. It was a warm day and the men welcomed lunchtime—they were hungry and thirsty.

Within fifteen minutes most of the group had eaten. Two men began to smoke, others talked in groups, and some sat quietly, waiting for the boss to check his watch. The moment of restful quietness was broken by a slamming door and the excited cries of children in a house above the roadway.

A five-year-old girl ran outside, screaming, "Mommy, Mommy, Ricky is trying to take my candy!" She dashed down the front steps of the house and started across the street where the road scraper sat. A boy, perhaps two years older than the girl, ran after her.

"There are the kids again!" the boss shouted, jumping to his feet. "How many times do I have to tell them to stay out of the street?"

For some unknown reason the entire group sensed the danger. Several men sprang to their feet and ran toward the hillside where the drilling machine stood.

Andy never knew how he got to his feet so quickly. As he told it later, he said the springs in his legs threw him into the air. He ran ahead of the boss shouting, "Go back! Go back!"

It all happened in seconds. The girl turned to meet the boy, stumbled, and fell down the hill, headfirst. The tiny body, with flying blonde hair and yellow dress, looked like a doll tumbling down the hillside. There was one scream of fright and pain. In a flash the child disappeared into one of the holes that had been dug that morning.

When the boy saw what had happened, he ran back toward the house crying wildly.

Andy got to the hole first. There was a prayer on his lips.

"No! No!" the boss cried, shaking his head and wringing his hands in disbelief.

Andy looked down. In the dim light he could see the child's head resting on her upturned knees. He called gently, "Are you all right, honey?"

There was no response.

The boss came to Andy's side groaning to himself, "Why didn't we think to cover the holes? This wouldn't have happened if the cement people had been on time!"

Stooping down, the boss called to the child two or three times. There was no answer. Then he jumped up and began to give orders quickly. He handed a man a car key, saying, "Mike, take my car. Get to a phone and call the sheriff's station and the fire department!"

At that moment a woman screamed and plunged down the hill. She was the child's mother. Her cries of alarm brought several women and a crowd of children from the other hillside homes.

The boss directed some of the workers to build a barricade[3] to hold back the gathering crowd.

The child's mother insisted on coming closer. She bent down on hands and knees and cried through her tears, "Carol! Carol! Are you all right? Oh, dear God, please save my baby!"

There was a flutter of life at the bottom of the hole.

"Mommy," the child cried.

"Are you all right, Carol?" the mother called again.

"My arm is hurted," the child said, and then she was quiet.

"You will be all right. . . . You will be all right," the mother repeated over and over. "The men will get you out in a hurry."

"Keep everybody back at least twenty feet!" the boss shouted. "I don't like the looks of the ground. If we have a cave-in, we'll never get her out alive!"

"I'll get a rope from the tool trailer," Andy suggested.

"Good. We'll try it," the boss said. "Tell Roy to bring the clamshell digger over here right away. Will the rest of you men lay some boards around the hole to work on."

In a few moments Andy was back with a thirty-foot coil of one-inch rope. Quickly he tied a loop in one end and bent to his knees on one of the boards. He lowered the rope and began to twirl[4] it gently. "Can you put the rope under your arms, honey?" he called.

There was no answer.

"Bring a flashlight," the boss called. "Quick!"

"Are you all right?" Andy called again.

There was no answer.

"Please, Carol," the mother pleaded. "Can't you answer? Please answer."

A worker handed the boss a flashlight. The light beam showed the child in a sitting position, with her head leaning against the side wall.

"Keep trying, Andy," the boss said. "If she raises her head for a moment, maybe you can get the rope around her body."

The fear of the awful danger overcame the mother. She cried out and fell to the ground in a faint.

II

Above the hum of voices, sirens sounded. A sheriff's car came up the street, followed immediately by a firetruck. A deputy sheriff and a fire chief hurried to where the boss stood. There was a hurried conference, followed by a nodding of heads.

The clamshell operator drove his machine within eight feet of the hole. The ground quivered as the heavy treads dug into the soft earth.

"Start digging," the boss ordered. "As soon as you are deep enough, we'll dig a lateral[5] tunnel to get her out."

At that moment Andy saw small bits of earth and gravel break loose inside the hole and rain to the bottom. "Take it easy!" he shouted. "There's a soft spot down there. We might have a cave-in."

"Stop the digger!" the fire chief exclaimed. "Let's get

this air hose down to her." He smiled with satisfaction when he saw the nozzle[6] of the hose pass by her head and drop below her body. "If she's alive, she'll be able to get some air even if the hole caves in," he said hopefully.

Just outside the police lines, a TV sound truck moved into position. On the top deck a man swung a camera into action while another man with a microphone moved about trying to get a newsstory.

Meanwhile the clamshell had dug a hole about six feet deep and about five feet in diameter. Then a frightful thing happened. The jaws of the digger scraped against a large boulder[7] in a useless effort. The operator tried again and groaned in disappointment when he realized that the machine could not dislodge the rock.

"Wait a moment," the boss said, grabbing a shovel and climbing down into the hole where the heavy rock showed through the dirt. He prodded and scraped for a minute and then shook his head. "You'll have to move the digger and start over. We'll never get around the rock."

Somehow the crowd sensed the bad news and there were cries of fear.

The boss looked at his watch nervously. The minutes had passed quickly and the hour was gone.

There was no time to lose! He estimated that with good luck the clamshell could reach the required depth within a half hour, but digging a lateral tunnel, most of it with hand tools, would take much longer. Other dangers lay ahead. He knew the soil in the whole area was unstable.[8]

Andy did not know anything about the reports of the soil tests that had been made several months earlier, but he did worry about the falling silt[9] every time the clamshell bit into the earth.

"Good boy, Andy!" the boss shouted. "Keep trying with the rope."

"Look," Andy replied, "her shoulders are already getting covered with dirt."

"Oh, God, we'll never make it!" the boss cried.

Overhearing the remarks, the TV broadcaster shouted into his microphone, "The hole is caving in! The child is already buried under falling dirt."

The clamshell operator increased the speed of his machine in a desperate hope. Each time the digger bit into the earth there was a jarring sound. Silt sifted from the bad spot and fell to the bottom, covering the child's hair.

III

With the flashlight Andy carefully examined the hole in which the child had been trapped. He turned to watch the digger a moment. Its progress seemed slow. He could see the outlines of little Carol's head and shoulders through the dirt that had been dislodged. [10]

Looking down into the hole, Andy thought to himself, "If my arms were only a little longer, I'd reach down and get you, little one." The thought brought back the memory of the day he dived into a hole of water at the beach trying to catch a lobster with his bare hands.

Suddenly Andy jumped to his feet and called to the boss. He spoke quietly but the boss kept shaking his head. Andy insisted firmly. The boss finally nodded his head and gave two orders. The clamshell operator stopped his machine. Another worker moved a small lifting crane up to a spot near the hole.

Meanwhile Andy, who was now sitting on the ground, was busy with the rope tying it into loops.

The crowd quieted. The TV broadcaster, sensing some new action, slipped past the police lines and began to question a deputy sheriff. Within the next two minutes TV viewers throughout the country watched a thrilling rescue attempt, step by step.

The cable on the crane began to turn. The crowd was amazed to see a slender youth hanging by his heels at the end of the crane. His body rested firmly in a rope net that

reached from his shoulders to his ankles, where the rope was attached to a wire cable.

"What's this? What's this?" a man called loudly.

A few guessed the truth when they saw Andy waving his arms in a signal. There was a murmur of disbelief when the crane lowered him into the hole, head down. Some people in the crowd of onlookers crossed themselves; others dropped to their knees in hopeful prayer.

The boss stood at the edge of the hole. He twirled his right hand in a signal. Slowly . . . slowly . . . the cable unwound from the drum that held it tightly. A few seconds escaped and time held still. There was a dead quiet. The boss stooped to his knees and held the flashlight as the cable unwound more slowly . . . now inch by inch. A muffled sound came from the hole. The boss smiled and raised the thumb of his right hand. A cheer rose from the crowd. The drum on the crane started reeling in the cable. Out of the pit Andy rose into the daylight. His long arms circled the shoulders of the child. Helping hands reached for her quickly. The man who took her was a doctor. There were several moments of fearful waiting. The TV broadcaster spoke into his microphone loud and clear: "This rescue effort is going to have a happy ending. The doctor says that little Carol is alive and unhurt. As you can see, this crowd has gone wild. And that applause you hear is for Andy Todd, the hero of this real-life drama."

• Building Your Vocabulary

1.	sole	single; only
2.	clamshell digger	a digging bucket hinged like a clamshell
3.	barricade	timbers placed to keep people away
4.	twirl	to whirl around
5.	lateral	coming from the side
6.	nozzle	the nose, or opening; a valve
7.	boulder	a large rock
8.	unstable	not firm; unsafe
9.	silt	loose dirt
10.	dislodged	made to fall; forced loose

• Exercises

A. Write the letter of the expression that best completes each of the following statements:
1. The main character in this story is _____.
    a. Andy   *b*. the fire chief   *c*. the boss
2. The person who got a flashlight from the tool trailer was _____.
    a. Andy   *b*. a deputy sheriff   *c*. a worker

3. The man who directed the rescue efforts was _____.
   a. a deputy sheriff
   b. the fire chief
   c. the boss
4. Besides himself, Andy's family consisted of his _____.
   a. mother and brother
   b. two brothers
   c. mother and little sister
5. Andy's mother worked during the afternoons _____.
   a. at a store
   b. at housecleaning
   c. at a laundry

B. Decide whether each of the following statements is true or false. Write T for *true* and F for *false*.
1. The holes Andy was drilling were about ten inches in diameter.
2. Andy operated a clamshell digger.
3. After the little girl fell into the hole, the boss got to the hole first.
4. The girl was wearing a yellow dress.
5. By using a flashlight, the boss was able to see the girl at the bottom of the hole.
6. After the girl fell into the hole, she never said a word until after she was rescued.
7. The boss told the workers to build a barricade to keep the people from crowding close to the hole.
8. Andy tried to get a rope around the girl's body.
9. The boss knew the soil in the area was unstable.
10. The TV broadcaster said that Andy was the hero of the rescue operation.

C. Write the letter of the definition in column II that most closely matches each expression in column I.

I. Word	**II. Definition**

I. Word

1. silt
2. nozzle
3. dislodged
4. sole
5. barricade
6. unstable
7. twirl
8. clamshell digger
9. lateral
10. boulder

II. Definition

A. a large rock
B. loose dirt
C. to whirl around
D. a digging bucket hinged like a clamshell
E. the nose, or opening; a valve
F. coming from the side
G. timbers placed to keep people away
H. made to fall; forced loose
I. not firm; unsafe
J. single; only

D. Write a paragraph or two on one of the following topics:

1. Describe the incident of the girl falling into the hole.
2. Discuss how the boss directed the rescue operations.
3. The TV broadcaster said that Andy was the hero. Try to prove or disprove this statement.
4. Have you ever seen an incident in which a person's life was in danger? Tell what happened.

God Sees
the Truth but Waits

Leo Tolstoy

I

"Ivan, don't go to the fair!" his wife begged. "I dreamed last night that you got into trouble while you were away, and then I saw that your hair had turned gray."

Ivan laughed. "That's a lucky sign," he said. "See if I don't sell all my goods and bring you some presents from the fair. What are you afraid of?"

His wife replied, "I don't know what I am afraid of. Please don't go."

Ivan smiled and said, "You are afraid that when I get to the fair, I shall go on a spree."[1]

Ivan Aksionov was a young merchant who lived in Vladimir. He had two shops and a house of his own. He was handsome, fair-haired, full of fun, and loved singing and playing the guitar. At one time he drank somewhat; but after he married, he gave up drinking.

"Don't worry," he said, "and you'll see that I'll bring you all the nice things I promised."

So Ivan got his wagon ready and drove away. He had gone about half way when darkness overtook him. He stopped at an inn for the night. There he met a merchant whom he knew. They had supper together and then talked awhile. At bedtime each went to his own room.

It was not Ivan's habit to sleep late, so early the next morning he paid his bill, hitched his horses to his wagon, and continued his journey.

When he had gone about ten miles, he stopped at an inn to get some food and have his horses fed. Then he ordered the samovar² to be heated for tea, stepped out onto the porch, got his guitar, and began to play.

Suddenly a troika³ drove up with tinkling bells. An official got down from the carriage, followed by two soldiers. Coming up to Ivan, the official began to question him, asking him who he was and where he lived.

Ivan answered the man fully and said, "Won't you have some tea with me?"

"Where did you stay last night?" the official asked. "Were you alone? Did you see another merchant this morning? Why did you leave so early?"

Ivan wondered why he was being asked so many questions, but he answered each one truthfully.

"Why do you ask me all these questions? I am not a thief or a robber. I am on my way to the fair on business."

Then the official said, "I am the police official of this district, and I question you because the merchant whom you visited with last night was found dead—murdered with a knife. We must search your things."

They entered the inn. The soldiers opened Ivan's luggage

and searched it. Suddenly the official drew a knife out of a bag and cried, "Whose knife is this?"

Ivan looked and, seeing a blood-stained knife, was frightened.

The official exclaimed, "There's blood on the knife! This knife is yours, isn't it?"

Ivan tried to answer. "The knife isn't mine," he said. "I have no idea how it got into my things. I know nothing about the death of the merchant."

Then the official replied, "This morning the merchant was found dead in his bed. You are the only person who could have done it. The inn was locked from the inside, and no one else could have done it. Here is the proof—a blood-stained knife in your luggage. Tell me how much money you stole."

Ivan swore that he had not done it, that he had not seen the merchant after they had had supper together, and that the knife was not his. But his voice broke in fear, and he trembled as though he were guilty.

The police official ordered the soldiers to truss[4] Ivan hand-and-foot and put him into a cart. As they tied his feet together, Ivan crossed himself and wept. His money and his goods were taken away from him, and he was sent to prison in the nearest town.

The police official began an investigation. The people in Vladmir said that Ivan used to drink and waste his time, but that he was now a good man. Then the trial came, and Ivan was charged [5] with the murder of the merchant and robbing him of his money.

Ivan's wife did not know what to believe. Taking her small children, she went to the town where her husband was in jail. At first she was not allowed to see him; but after much begging, she got a permit and was taken to him. When she saw her husband in prison dress and in chains, she fell down in a faint.

Finally coming to her senses, she drew her children near and asked him what had happened.

He told her all he knew. Then she asked, "What can we do now?"

"We must petition[6] the czar[7] not to let an innocent man perish."

His wife then told him that she had already sent a petition to the czar and that it had not been accepted.

Then his wife said, "It was not for nothing that I had

the strange dream about you. You should not have gone that day. Tell your wife the truth; was it not you who did it?"

"Oh, God in heaven, you don't believe me!" he exclaimed. Then he began to weep. A guard came to say it was time for his family to leave.

When they were gone, Ivan remembered what his wife had said, and he thought to himself, "It seems that only God can know the truth; and it is to Him we must now go for help."

Ivan gave up all hope that the officials would listen to him. He was condemned[8] to be flogged,[9] and then he was driven to Siberia with six other convicts.

II

Ivan was no longer happy. His hair had turned gray in a short time, and he no longer enjoyed playing the guitar. He never laughed or sang but he prayed often.

The prison officials in Siberia could not believe he had ever done anything wrong. His fellow prisoners liked him and they called him "Grandfather." He helped them with their problems and he became a counselor to many of the men.

During the time that he was in prison, Ivan did not hear from home. He did not know anything about his wife or his children.

Then a strange thing happened. One day more convicts were brought to the prison. One of the new prisoners was Makar, a tall, strong man of sixty with a gray beard. He said he had been accused of stealing a horse. He bragged about the fact that he had been in prison before. He said he didn't stay long in a prison—he knew how to get out, and he was planning to be on his way soon.

"Where are you from?" one of the prisoners asked.

"From Vladmir. My family live in that town," he replied.

Ivan raised his head and asked, "Tell me, Makar, do you know anything about the Aksionov family?"

"Know them? Of course, I do. They are rich though I heard that Ivan Aksionov had been sent to prison. He was a sinner like ourselves, I guess. Tell me, Granddad, why are you here?"

Ivan did not tell. He only sighed and said, "I have been sent here for my sins."

"What sins?" Makar asked.

Ivan did not reply.

Some of the other prisoners told Makar how someone had killed a merchant and had placed the knife among Ivan's things.

When Makar heard this, he looked at Ivan, slapped his knee, and exclaimed, "Well, this is strange. He has surely grown old in a hurry."

The others asked Makar if he had ever seen Ivan before.

Makar acted strangely and would not make a direct reply. He only said, "It's strange that we should meet here, lads!"

Makar was acting so strangely that Ivan wondered if he knew who killed the merchant. Then he said, "Perhaps, Makar, you have heard of the affair, or maybe you've seen me before?"

"Of course, I've heard of the affair. The world is full of rumors. But it's a long time ago, and I've forgotten what I heard."

"Perhaps you heard who killed the merchant?" Ivan asked.

Makar laughed and replied, "It must have been the man in whose bag the knife was found. How could anyone put a knife in your bag while it was under your head without waking you?"

When Ivan heard these words, he was sure it was Makar who had killed the man. How else would he know so many facts?

Ivan rose and walked away, feeling sad. He remembered his wife, his children, and how happy he had been with his family. He remembered how he used to play the guitar and sing; and then he remembered his arrest, the trial, the flogging, the chains, and the long trip to Siberia. At that moment Ivan wished he were dead.

"He's the murderer!" Ivan said to himself, but he had no way to prove his own innocence. He could only hope and pray. He knew that God knew the truth—and the truth could not be hidden forever. He was so troubled that he could not sleep at night.

One night as he walked along a long room where the prisoners slept, he saw some earth rolling out from under one of the shelfbeds set against the wall. Stopping to see what it was, he saw Makar crawl out from under the bed.

Ivan attempted to pass on without saying anything, but Makar grabbed him by the hand and held him fast. He told Ivan that he was digging a hole beyond the wall and that each day he carried the dirt out in his boots when the prisoners were driven to their work.

"Just keep quiet, old man," Makar said, "and don't say anything. If they find out, they'll flog the life out of me, but I'll kill you first!"

Ivan felt afraid. "I have no wish to escape," he said, "and you need not kill me. You did that a long time ago."

The next day when the prisoners were led out to work, a guard caught Makar pouring dirt out of his boots. The prison was searched and the tunnel found.

The prison governor tried to find out who had dug the tunnel. Every prisoner denied having any knowledge of the tunnel. At last the governor turned to Ivan, and said, "You are a truthful man. Tell me who dug the hole."

Ivan bit his lip and thought to himself, "Why should I protect Makar? He ruined my life. Let him pay for the suffering he caused me. . . . Well, maybe I am wrong in thinking he put the knife into my bag. If I tell, they'll flog the life out of him."

"Well," the governor said, "tell me the truth! Do you know who has been digging that hole?"

Ivan said quietly, "I cannot say. It's not God's will that I tell. Do what you will with me."

The governor tried again, but Ivan had nothing more to say.

That night after Ivan had gone to bed, he heard someone in the darkness approaching his bed. He knew it was Makar. "What do you want?" he asked Makar.

For a moment Makar was silent.

Ivan sat up and said, "What do you want? Go away or I'll call the guard!"

Makar bent his head and said quietly, "Ivan Aksionov, forgive me!"

"What for?" Ivan asked.

"It was I who killed the merchant and hid the knife among your things. I meant to take your money too, but I heard a noise outside, and I jumped out the window and ran."

Ivan was silent and did not know what to say.

Then Makar began to plead. "Forgive me, forgive me for the love of God!" he said. "I will confess that I killed the merchant, and you will go free."

"It is easy to talk," Ivan said, "but I have suffered a long time. Where could I go now? My wife may be dead and my children have probably forgotten me."

Makar did not rise. "Ivan, forgive me!" he cried. "When they flogged me with the knout,[10] it was not so hard to bear as it is to see you now, an old forgotten man. In God's name, forgive me!"

When Ivan heard Makar pleading, he, too, began to weep.

"God will forgive you!" Ivan said. "In my heart I have no hatred or desire for revenge."

"Thank you, old man," Makar said. "God has made me

see the light. I know that the truth cannot be hidden forever. You will be a free man soon, for tomorrow I shall tell the governor the truth about the merchant."

• *Building Your Vocabulary*

1.	spree	a period of drinking
2.	samovar	a container used for making tea
3.	troika	a vehicle drawn by three horses abreast
4.	truss	to tie firmly
5.	charged	accused of a crime
6.	petition	to plead for help; to beg
7.	czar	a Russian emperor
8.	condemned	sentenced to be punished
9.	flogged	beaten severely with a whip
10.	knout	a whip for beating criminals

• *Exercises*

A. Write an expression that would complete each sentence correctly.

1. Ivan laughed. "That's a lucky _____," he said.
2. When Ivan had gone about ten miles, he stopped at an _____ to get some food and have his horses fed.
3. The police officer ordered the soldiers to tie Ivan hand-and-foot and put him into a _____.
4. Ivan was sent to a prison in _____.
5. All the prisoners liked Ivan, and they called him _____.

B. Decide whether each of the following statements is true or false. Write T for *true* and F for *false*.

1. Ivan loved to play the guitar.
2. Ivan's wife warned him not to go to the fair.
3. The soldiers found the knife in Ivan's wagon.

4. Ivan's wife sent a petition to the czar asking for Ivan's release.
5. The prison officials in Siberia believed that Ivan was guilty.
6. During the time he was in prison, Ivan never heard from home.
7. Makar said he had heard of Ivan's family.
8. Ivan gave up praying to God for help.
9. Ivan never once thought that it was Makar who had killed the merchant.
10. Ivan told the prison governor that Makar was digging an escape tunnel.

C. Write the letter of the definition in column II that most closely matches each word in column I.

I. Word   ### II. Definition

1. knout   A. a period of drinking
2. spree   B. a vehicle drawn by three horses
3. samovar   abreast
4. truss   C. a Russian emperor
5. czar   D. a container used for making tea
6. condemned   E. a whip for beating criminals
7. troika   F. beaten severely with a whip
8. charged   G. accused of a crime
9. flogged   H. to plead for help; to beg
10. petition   I. to tie firmly
                J. sentenced to be punished

D. Write a paragraph or two on one of the following topics:
1. Tell what happened at the inn the night that the merchant was killed. Try to prove that Ivan was innocent.

2 . Tell what happened to Ivan after he was arrested by the police official.

3 . Describe the kind of person Ivan was at the beginning of the story and tell how he changed.

4 . Tell how Ivan came to know that it was Makar who killed the merchant.

Jimmy Valentine

O. Henry

I

A guard came to the prison shoeshop, where Jimmy was working, and told him that the warden[1] wished to see him.

Jimmy went into the warden's office, not knowing what to expect.

"Valentine," the warden said, "you'll be pleased to hear that the governor has given you a pardon.[2] You'll go out in the morning. . . . Brace up and make a man of yourself. You are not a bad fellow at heart. Stop cracking safes and live straight."

"Me?" Jimmy said, in surprise. "Why, I never cracked a safe in my life."

"Oh, no," the warden laughed. "Of course not. Let's see now. How was it you happened to get sent up on that Springfield job? Was it because you couldn't prove an alibi?[3] Or was it simply a case of a mean jury that had it in for you?"

"Me?" Jimmy said. "Why, warden, I was never in Springfield in my life."

"Take him away," the warden said. "Release him at seven tomorrow morning. Better think over my advice, Valentine."

At seven o'clock the next morning Jimmy Valentine was in the warden's outer office, waiting for the door to be unlocked. He wore a badly fitting ready-made suit and a pair of stiff shoes the state provides its discharged[4] guests.

The clerk handed him a railroad ticket and a five-dollar bill that was supposed to help him get a new start in life. The warden gave him a cigar, shook his hand, and wished him well.

Jimmy walked slowly to the railroad station. On the way he tossed a quarter into the hat of a blind man sitting by a doorway.

Three hours later he left the train at a little station near the state line. He went to the café of one Mike Dolan and shook hands with Mike, who was alone behind the bar.

"Sorry we couldn't get you out sooner, Jimmy, me boy," Mike said. "The governor, you know, wasn't sure about you. Are you all right?"

"Fine," Jimmy said. "Do you have my key?"

Mike handed over the key. Jimmy went upstairs and unlocked the door of a room at the rear. Everything was just as he had left it. On the floor he found one of Ben Price's cuff links, which had been dropped when that eminent[5] detective had arrested him.

Pulling from the wall a folding bed, Jimmy slid back a panel in the wall and dragged out a dust-covered suitcase. He opened it and gazed fondly at the finest set of burglar tools in the East. It was a complete set, and it had cost him over nine hundred dollars.

In half an hour Jimmy went downstairs through the café. He was now dressed in tasteful, well-fitting clothes and carried his dusted and cleaned suitcase in his hand.

"Got anything on?" Mike Dolan asked.

"Me?" Jimmy said in a puzzled tone. "I don't understand. I'm now an honest salesman, representing the New York Snappy Cracker Company."

A week after the release of Valentine, there was a neat safe burglary in Indiana and then there was a bank safe robbery in Missouri. The losses were high, and the police and the bank officials decided to ask for the help of the famous thief-catcher Ben Price.

"It looks like Jimmy Valentine again," he said after he had completed his investigation.[6] "He's up to his old tricks, I'll bet."

One afternoon Jimmy climbed down from a mail coach in Elmore, a little town in the back country of Arkansas. Jimmy, looking like an athletic young senior just home from college, went down the board sidewalk toward the hotel.

A young lady crossed the street, passed him at the corner and entered a door over which hung the sign "The Elmore Bank." Jimmy looked into her eyes, forgot what he was, and became another man. She looked at Jimmy and blushed. Young men of Jimmy's style and looks were scarce in Elmore.

Jimmy spoke to a boy who was loafing in front of the bank. "Isn't that Miss Polly Simpson?" he asked.

"Naw," the boy said. "She's Annabel Adams. Her pa owns this bank."

Jimmy was forced to make a quick decision. He had fallen in love with Miss Annabel Adams.

He went to the hotel and registered as Ralph D. Spencer. He told the clerk he had come to Elmore to start a business. He had thought of a shoe business. Was there an opening?

The clerk was impressed with Jimmy's style. He liked Jimmy's new bow tie. Yes, there was need for a shoe store in town, and he hoped Mr. Spencer would locate there soon.

And so, Mr. Ralph Spencer put aside all that was Jimmy Valentine and became a good citizen of Elmore. His store did well from the beginning. Meanwhile he had become socially popular in the town. He had met Annabel Adams, and before the end of the year they were engaged.

II

Jimmy's star of fortune had begun to shine brightly. But he worried how he could get rid of the ugly contents of the suitcase he kept locked in a closet in his hotel room. He knew he would never wrongly take another dollar as long as he lived. Finally he had a bright idea: he would drive over to Little Rock and order his wedding suit and get some nice things for Annabel. On the way he would toss the tools into weed patches and deep ditches; and returning, he would have only the things he intended to buy.

On the same morning that Jimmy planned to leave, Ben Price drove into town. He walked about the streets in his quiet way until he found out what he wanted to know. From the drug store across the street he had a good look at Ralph D. Spencer as he came out of his shoe store. Jimmy was on his way to have breakfast with the Adams family. He carried a suitcase. He had already engaged a horse and buggy at the livery stable[7] just around the corner from the bank.

"Going to marry the banker's daughter, are you, Jimmy?" Price said to himself softly. "Well, you may have to change your plans."

After breakfast quite a family party went downtown together—Mr. Adams, Annabel, Jimmy, and Annabel's married sister with her two little girls, aged five and nine. All went inside the high, carved oak railings into the banking room—Jimmy included, for Mr. Adams' future son-in-law was welcome anywhere.

Jimmy set his suitcase down. There weren't many customers in the bank that morning. The going-away party caused quite a bit of excitement.

Excited and happy, Annabel put on Jimmy's hat and picked up the suitcase. "Wouldn't I make a nice salesman?" Annabel said. "My, Ralph, how heavy it is! Feels like it is full of gold bricks."

"Just some junk I'm going to get rid of," Jimmy said.

The Elmore Bank had just put in a new walk-in vault. Mr. Adams was very proud of it, and he insisted on showing it to everyone. The door had three solid steel bolts and a combination lock and a time clock. Mr. Adams explained its workings to Jimmy, who didn't seem to have much interest in it. The two children, May and Ellen, were delighted with the shining metal, the funny clock, and the knobs that turned.

During all this excitement, Ben Price came into the bank and leaned against a rail. He told a clerk he didn't want anything; he was just waiting for a man he knew.

Suddenly there was a scream or two from the women. May, the older girl, in the spirit of play, had shut Ellen in the vault. She had then turned the knobs as she had seen Mr. Adams do.

The old banker sprang to the handle and tugged at it. "The door can't be opened," he groaned. "The clock hasn't been wound nor the combination set."

Ellen's mother screamed.

"Hush!" Mr. Adams said, raising his trembling hand. "Ellen," he called as loudly as he could. "Listen to me." During the following silence they could just hear the faint sound of the child shrieking in terror.

"Oh, Ellen," the mother cried. "She will die of fright. Open the door! Oh, break it open! Can't you men do something?"

"There isn't a man nearer than Little Rock who can open that door," Mr. Adams said. "She can't live long in there. There isn't enough air!"

Ellen's mother began to beat the vault with her hands. Somebody wildly suggested dynamite. Annabel turned to Jimmy. To a woman nothing seems impossible to the powers of a man whom she loves.

"Can't you do something, Ralph—try, won't you?" she begged.

He looked at her with a soft smile on his lips. Then he bent forward and kissed her gently on the cheek. With that act Ralph D. Spencer passed away, and once again he was Jimmy Valentine. Then he took off his jacket and rolled up his sleeves. He knew without a doubt that this would be his last job as a safecracker.

"Get away from the door, all of you!" he commanded.

He set his suitcase by the vault and opened it out flat. He laid out the shining, strange tools swiftly and quietly. For a moment he smiled when he saw how carefully he had arranged the tools in order. And then his expression[8] changed to one of deep concern.[9] In silence the others watched him as if under a spell.

In a minute Jimmy's pet drill was biting smoothly into the steel door. In less than ten minutes—breaking his own record—he threw back the bolts and opened the door.

Ellen, almost suffocated,[10] was gathered into the arms of her mother.

Jimmy Valentine put on his jacket and walked toward the front door. As he went he thought he heard a far-away voice he once knew calling to him, "Ralph! Ralph!" But he never stopped.

At the door Ben Price stood somewhat in his way.

"Hello, Ben," Jimmy said with a strange smile. "I see you finally got around. . . . Well, let's go. I don't think it makes any difference, now."

And then Ben Price acted rather strangely. He stepped back from the doorway.

"Guess you are mistaken, sir," he said. "I don't believe

I know you. That was a remarkable thing you just did. You should get a medal."

Ben Price turned and walked away.

Again, Jimmy heard someone calling, "Ralph!" This time the voice seemed closer—and pleading.

As he turned around, Annabel rushed toward him. "Where are you going?" she cried.

"I . . . I don't know," he said. "I was afraid our plans had come to an end . . . after what you saw."

"Don't be silly!" she exclaimed tearfully. "Nothing has changed. I love you more than ever."

"Oh, Annabel, thank God!" Jimmy cried, as he took both her hands in his.

"Do you have to go to Little Rock?" she asked.

"Yes . . . yes, I have important business to take care of. I'll be back."

"Is that a promise?" she asked.

"That is a promise, my love," Jimmy replied happily.

"I'll be waiting," Annabel said, as Jimmy kissed her tenderly.

• *Building Your Vocabulary*

1.	warden	a person in charge of a prison
2.	pardon	an official paper freeing a prisoner
3.	alibi	an excuse; a plea of being elsewhere at the time of a crime
4.	discharged	let go or freed
5.	eminent	outstanding; superior
6.	investiga-tion	study
7.	livery stable	a place where horses and carriages are kept for hire
8.	expression	the look on one's face
9.	concern	seriousness; worry
10.	suffocated	choked; smothered

• *Exercises*

A. Write an expression that would complete each sentence correctly.

1. The _____ told Jimmy to brace up and make a man of himself.
2. The eminent detective was _____.
3. Jimmy's suitcase contained _____.
4. In the story Elmore is in the state of _____.
5. After he came to Elmore, Jimmy changed his name to _____.

B. Decide whether each of the following statements is true or false. Write T for *true* and F for *false*.

1. The warden said to Jimmy, "You are not a bad fellow at heart."
2. Jimmy told the warden that he had never cracked a safe in his life.
3. The prison clerk gave Jimmy ten dollars.
4. The first time Jimmy saw Annabel Adams he fell in love with her.
5. There weren't many young men in Elmore who had Jimmy's style and looks.
6. In Elmore Jimmy worked as a clerk in a shoe store.
7. Ben Price suspected Jimmy of some robberies after Jimmy had been let out of prison.
8. Mr. Adams, Annabel's father, was a banker.
9. After falling in love with Annabel, Jimmy no longer wanted the burglar tools he kept in his suitcase.
10. After he saw Jimmy open the bank safe at Elmore, Ben Price took Jimmy back to jail.

C. Write the letter of the definition in column II that most closely matches each expression in column I.

I. Word	II. Definition
1. suffocated	A. an official paper freeing a prisoner
2. eminent	B. the look on one's face
3. expression	C. choked; smothered
4. pardon	D. a place where horses and carriages
5. concern	are kept for hire
6. investiga-	E. let go or freed
tion	F. a person in charge of a prison
7. livery	G. seriousness; worry
stable	H. an excuse; a plea of being elsewhere
8. warden	at the time of a crime
9. alibi	I. outstanding; superior
10. discharged	J. study

D. Write a paragraph or two on one of the following topics:

1. Describe the last meeting Jimmy Valentine had with the prison warden.
2. What event changed Jimmy? Tell how he changed.
3. Tell how Jimmy rescued the little girl from the vault.
4. Tell what would have happened if Ben Price had taken Jimmy back to jail.

Fasten Seat Belts

Ralph V. Cutlip

I

The big 707 jet climbed into the air with a roar of its mighty engines. Behind the plane the runway faded into a thin line in the morning haze. In a few seconds the passengers saw below them the dancing surf of the Pacific Ocean.

Suddenly the loudspeaker was turned on with a metallic click. A man's voice came through loud and clear: "Good morning, ladies and gentlemen. This is the captain. We are now at six thousand feet. To your right is Catalina Island, and in the distance is San Clemente Island. In a few seconds we will be turning inland just north of Oceanside. Our flight plan this morning is almost a beeline to Miami by way of Phoenix, El Paso, Houston, and across the Gulf of Mexico. The trip looks like a smooth one all the way. We will be flying at an altitude of 37,000 feet. Have a nice day."

There was another click of the loudspeaker, and the plane

34

was quiet except for the drone[1] of the powerful engines and the low hum of voices.

Within five minutes, Betty Kingman, the first stewardess, made her way down the aisle of the first-class compartment[2] and the coach section, getting the names of the passengers on her flight list.

Betty had a smile and a calmness that showed her self-confidence. She was of average height, and the light blue uniform accented her velvety features. Her cap rested gently on her pageboy hairdo. Her blonde hair blended[3] with the gentle warmth and beauty of her pale blue eyes.

Making a passenger list was just one of Betty's many duties.

II

A few seconds before, Betty and the second stewardess, Marie Martinez, had stood at the doorway, welcoming the passengers aboard and checking their tickets.

It was like any other day for Betty except for two passengers who got her attention in unusual ways. The first was a man of about thirty-five, of dark complexion, with bushy sideburns.

"Guess I'll go with you to Miami," he said with a nervous grin.

Betty forced a smile and said, "Welcome aboard."

Part of her training had been to be alert for danger signs of any kind. As the man passed into the cabin, she frowned to herself. Two danger signals had flashed. The man was nervous to the point of trembling. His eyes had a strange, faraway look. And she was sure he had been drinking quite a bit—probably in the effort to steady his nerves. She wondered if he was sick.

He was dressed neatly in gray slacks, with a dark blue jacket. His tie was patterned in red, gold, and blue stripes. In his right hand he carried a flight bag. The strap of a camera case looped over his chest and right shoulder. He could well have been taken for just another tourist.

The last passenger aboard was an elderly woman who had come along the walkway in slowed step, clutching her purse in her left hand and a cane in her right. Where her right hand held the cane, her fingers pinched a ticket envelope tightly.

"Welcome aboard," Betty said.

The woman forced a smile. She was frightened. "I have two pills to take," she said. "My doctor thought they would help."

"You'll be just fine," Betty said. "Miss Martinez will show you to your seat."

The second stewardess took the ticket envelope, looked at the seat number written on the outside, and said, "Come, I'll show you the way."

"This is my first trip by air," the woman said. "I guess I am a little scared."

"You haven't a thing to worry about," Marie replied. "Be sure to fasten your seat belt. Do you want some water?"

"No, thank you," the woman said. "I don't need any water to swallow a couple of little pills."

Betty stepped back from the open doorway when a warning light flashed and a buzzer sounded.

The boarding ramp[4] pulled away, and then the door closed quietly.

The warning lights flashed—Fasten Seat Belts. The jet engines screamed, and the plane began to taxi toward the head of the flight strip.

As the stewardesses moved down the aisle, checking to see that all the passengers had secured their safety belts,

Betty was somewhat surprised to find the elderly woman sitting in the same row as the man.

She was next to the window. He sat nearest to the aisle, leaving a vacant seat between them. His flight bag and his camera lay half hidden under the vacant seat.

The woman was fumbling helplessly with her seat belt, trying to fasten it.

"Pardon me, sir," Betty said.

Showing some politeness, the man rose to his feet to allow her to sit in the second seat for a moment. She showed the woman how to bring the ends of the belt together and lock them in place. Then she showed her how to unfasten the belt. It took only a few seconds, and Betty was back in the aisle checking other passengers.

By this time the plane had taxied to the head of the flight runway and had turned around. The engines roared, and the great plane strained at the brakes that held it fast to the ground.

The flight signal came from the tower, and the plane shot down the runway and became airborne[5] in a few seconds.

III

By the time Betty had finished her passenger list, the second stewardess had started the movie film.

Most of the passengers began to watch the film with interest. A few dozed, and some gazed out the window at the earth below, where it lay like a picture.

Suddenly Betty saw that the man was becoming restless. He made two trips down the aisle, once to the water cooler and then to the lavatory. Twice he looked at his wristwatch. When he returned from the lavatory, he walked past his own seat and wandered through the first-class compartment up to the door of the cockpit.[6] She saw him peering through the glass door panel, and she spoke to him quietly, "Coach area, please."

Time passed quickly. Before the film had finished screening, the stewardess had served drinks to those who wished them. Then they passed out the menus and began to pick up the orders for lunch. Their busiest hour came when they started bringing the food trays from the kitchen.

The work of serving lunch continued at a busy pace as the stewardesses brought more coffee, tea, and milk from the kitchen. Then the girls moved down the aisle to collect the empty food trays.

As Betty reached to take a tray, the woman with the cane unbuckled her seat belt and asked in a trembling voice, "Where is the rest room?"

"Back there. I'll show you," Betty said.

The man stepped into the aisle to let the woman out.

"I haven't been on a plane before," the woman said, winking and hiding her smile of embarrassment behind her hand.

The man dropped back into his seat. He reached down quickly and opened the zipper on his flight bag. Then he pulled out onto the floor a badly wrinkled map and a paperback book. Somewhere in the bag he found a writing tablet. Holding the tablet on his knees, he began to write rapidly.

When Betty came back down the aisle, the man reached his hand toward her. "Give this to the captain!" he commanded. "It is important."

She took the note calmly, but her fears began to rise. She knew there was no security officer[7] aboard her flight. Had there been one, she would have met him before boarding the plane. Then the officer would have come aboard like any other passenger. She knew there was only one thing she could do—take the note to the captain.

Reaching the door of the cockpit, she handed the note

through the door to the second officer.

She waited a few minutes. It seemed like an hour. The door opened, and she was told to step inside.

"I'm afraid we have a hijacker aboard," the captain said. "Maybe he's some kind of nut. Says he wants to go to Cuba . . . says he has a gun, and he will use it if he has to . . . says everybody can get off the plane at Miami except the crew. Keep an eye on him. I'm going to call Houston. I'll think of something."

"What can I do?" Betty asked.

"Nothing," the captain replied. "Just tell him we'll go on to Havana after we land at Miami. If he starts up here, try to talk him out of it—but don't get in his way. And don't ask for help. Can you describe him?"

Quickly Betty described the man, giving his height, possible weight, and most important, a description of his clothes. Then she walked back down the aisle, passing through the curtain that separated the first-class compartment from the coach section.

When she got back to where the man sat, he looked up and said, "Well?"

"The captain said Yes. Let's keep our voices down," Betty replied. "No use frightening these people."

"I don't want to harm anybody," the man said. "Just do as I say and nobody will get hurt."

At that moment the woman returned to her seat. The man rose to his feet quickly and stepped aside. Once again Betty sensed his fear and his nervousness. She handed the lady her cane and stepped back. The man was gone. She saw him disappear into one of the lavatories.

Betty took one more glance to see that the woman passenger was seated comfortably. Then she saw something that made her nerves tingle. The flight bag had been left partly open. From under a mussed shirt, the handle of a revolver showed.

She acted quickly. Nothing told her what to do or how to do it. With one quick movement she pulled the gun out of the bag and rolled it up in a paper dinner napkin that lay almost under the woman's feet.

"What are you doing, honey?" the woman asked.

"Just picking up," Betty replied. "Now . . . are you all right?"

"Just fine. Thank you for your kindness," the woman answered. "I guess I'm no longer scared. This is fun!"

"You are a good passenger," Betty said, as she turned and walked toward the kitchen. In her hand she carried the soiled napkin. Reaching the kitchen, she dropped the gun into a garbage container.

All this action took place so quickly that the other stewardess was not aware of what had happened. As a matter of fact, she did not know that the plane was being threatened by a hijacker. Marie was new—just out of training school—and Betty thought it would be unwise to tell her. Inexperienced as she was, the new stewardess might make a mistake that would cause panic among the passengers.

Betty signaled the captain. Again the second officer opened the door. Betty told the captain what had happened. He frowned and then smiled. "Maybe it's a real break that he didn't have the gun on his person. It was a dangerous thing for you to do. We're already in touch with the F.B.I. in Houston and in Miami. Play it cool. Maybe we can work out something up here."

"I wonder what he will do if he finds out the gun is gone," Betty said to herself quietly.

IV

Betty helped the second stewardess collect the rest of the food trays. Soon the plane would be passing Houston and crossing the blue waters of the Gulf of Mexico. In little more than an hour it would be in Miami.

The man returned to his seat. He picked up the map and the paperback book and shoved them back into his flight bag.

Seven minutes out of Houston the jet engines suddenly slowed to three-fourths of the normal cruising[8] power. Even the passengers noted the change in the forward motion of the plane. Then the engines caught up at full force, and the plane picked up speed. Ten seconds passed, and again the engines cut down. The plane slowed to a landing speed.

Some of the passengers began to look about nervously.

"Are we stopping?" a woman asked, tugging at Betty's sleeve.

"Perhaps. We'll know in a moment," Betty answered quite calmly.

"Are we in some kind of trouble?" a man asked.

"I am sure everything is all right," Betty said, smiling at him.

Suddenly the sign flashed—*Fasten Seat Belts.*

The loudspeaker turned on with a scratchy sound: "This is the captain. We have a little emergency. There is no danger. I repeat—there is no danger. We are having some trouble with a fuel line. We'll land in Houston in a few minutes. You will transfer to another plane for Miami. I am sorry for the inconvenience. I repeat—there is no danger. You know we don't take chances."

The plane picked up normal speed.

Betty smiled to herself in a knowing way. She felt she was able to guess what had happened.

Again the engines cut to a landing speed, and the plane turned slightly to position[9] itself on the landing beam.

Betty and the second stewardess took empty seats and fastened their seat belts. Betty breathed a little more easily when she looked out the window and saw the braking flaps open up along the back edge of the wing. Down . . . down

. . . the huge plane swept to the edge of the runway, touching the ground as smoothly as a drifting feather. Then the plane turned off the main runway and rolled to a stop.

Again the captain's voice came over the loudspeaker: "All passengers will please leave the plane here. The trams[10] will take you and your luggage to a waiting plane. Thank you."

Before the passengers had unbuckled their seat belts and had secured their personal belongings, Betty and the second stewardess hurried to their stations at the exit door.

The door opened, and a portable stairway nosed into place.

Betty looked down, expecting to see several police cars and a swarm of police and F.B.I. agents. There was none. A man in the uniform of an airport attendant stood at the bottom of the stairway smiling.

A stream of passengers came down the aisle and began to descend the steps. The man at the bottom of the stairway reached out a hand now and then to assist an elderly passenger to the ground.

Already the plane luggage compartment had been opened, and uniformed attendants hurried to transfer the luggage containers to the trams.

Betty was suddenly conscious of a voice at her elbow.

"Thank you again, honey," the woman said. "This is sure an exciting way to travel."

"Glad you enjoyed the trip," Betty replied. Then she began to wonder where the hijacker was. She turned to see him looking out a window of the first-class compartment.

In another moment he stood at her side. Again the strap of his camera case was looped over his shoulder, and he carried the bulging flight bag under his left arm. The zipper was half open, and Betty shuddered, surprised that he had not missed the gun.

"I'll follow you and the rest of the crew," he said. "Call them."

Betty stepped to the door of the cockpit and called.

The other crew members came out, unsmiling and looking serious.

On a motion from the hijacker, they started down the steps. The captain was last in line, followed by the hijacker. The moment the hijacker stepped onto the ground, the attendant at the bottom of the stairway seized him by the right arm. Another attendant stepped around the corner of the stairway and took hold of the hijacker's left arm.

There was no struggle; there was no outcry of surprise.

"This way," the attendant said quietly. "We're with the F.B.I. You are now under arrest."

Less than a half dozen people saw the hijacker being led away. There were two or three cries of surprise.

"What was all that about?" one man on the tram asked.

"I haven't the faintest idea," a woman replied, "but he looks like the man who sat across the aisle from me. I'll bet he's wanted for something."

As the two stewardesses climbed aboard a tram, Betty said, "Well, I guess the captain did think of something."

"What's that?" Marie asked, somewhat puzzled.

"I'll tell you sometime," Betty said with a smile.

• Building Your Vocabulary

1.	**drone**	a humming sound
2.	**compartment**	a separate section
3.	**blended**	combined well
4.	**ramp**	a sloping passageway
5.	**airborne**	supported by the air
6.	**cockpit**	the space in an airplane used by pilots and flight officers
7.	**security officer**	a guard
8.	**cruising**	being used when flying normally
9.	**position**	to place
10.	**trams**	vehicles used to transport passengers

● *Exercises*

A. Write an expression that would complete each sentence correctly.

1. The plane was flying to Miami by way of Phoenix, El Paso, and _____.
2. The last passenger aboard was an elderly _____.
3. Besides a camera case, the man carried a _____.
4. Reaching the door of the cockpit, Betty handed the note to the _____.
5. Seven minutes out of Houston the jet engines suddenly slowed to three-fourths of the normal _____.

B. Decide whether each of the following statements is true or false. Write T for *true* and F for *false*.

1. The plane was a 747 jet.
2. After the plane first took off, the passengers could see the Pacific Ocean below them.
3. The captain said the plane would be flying at an altitude of 35,000 feet.
4. One of Betty's jobs was to make a passenger list.
5. The elderly woman with the cane said she had never been on a plane before.
6. The hijacker asked Betty for some writing paper.
7. Betty took the hijacker's note to a security officer.
8. Betty hid the hijacker's gun in a garbage container.
9. The plane made a stop at El Paso.
10. When the plane arrived at the Houston airport, Betty expected to see a swarm of police and F.B.I. agents.

C. Write a paragraph or two on one of the following topics:

1. Tell about the work Betty had to do as an airline stewardess.
2. Describe the hijacker and tell what he tried to do.
3. Tell how the hijacker was captured.

4. Imagine you were the captain of the plane. Tell how you helped to trick the hijacker.

D. Write the letter of the definition in column II that most closely matches each expression in column I.

I. Word	II. Definition
1. position	A. a humming sound
2. drone	B. a guard
3. compart-ment	C. vehicles used to transport passengers
	D. supported by the air
4. cockpit	E. a sloping passageway
5. trams	F. flying normally
6. blended	G. to place
7. cruising	H. combined well
8. ramp	I. the space in an airplane used by the pilots and flight officers
9. security officer	
	J. a separate section
10. airborne	

The Costume Jewelry

Guy de Maupassant

I

Emil Lantin had fallen in love with Jeanine the first time he saw her. He had met her at a party at the home of the chief of the government department where he worked.

She was the daughter of a country doctor who had died several months earlier. Her mother had brought her to Paris in the hope of making a good marriage for her.

The young girl seemed the type of sensible person every young man dreams of one day winning for a wife. She was beautiful and she was charming. She was praised by everybody who knew her. People were never tired of saying: "It will be a lucky man who wins her love."

Emil had a fair income, and he thought he could safely support a wife and maintain a home for her. He proposed and was accepted.

He was quite content with his marriage. She took good care of their home, and they lived quite happily together.

47

As time went by, he could find only two faults: her love for the theater and her taste for fine clothing and jewelry. Her friends often got her a box at the theater, and her husband went along although he felt tired after a day's work at the office.

After a time, Emil begged his wife to get some lady friend to go with her instead of him. She at first opposed this arrangement, but she finally consented—much to his delight although he loved his wife.

Now with her love for the theater came the desire to adorn[1] herself with costume jewelry. True, her clothes remained as before, in good taste; but she had soon acquired many pieces of jewelry, some of which sparkled like real diamonds. Around her neck she wore a pearl necklace, and on her arms bracelets of imitation gold. When she bought a new dress, she would frequently ask her husband to buy a piece of costume jewelry to go with it—a pin, a bracelet, or a necklace.

"Why do you want all that stuff?" he would ask.

"It's nice to have variety," she would answer sweetly.

Her husband scolded her, saying, "My dear, as we can't afford real diamonds, you shouldn't wear imitation jewelry. You already have a natural beauty and modesty, the most valuable of all jewels."

But she would smile lovingly and say: "What can I do? I'm so fond of jewelry. I can't change my nature. My grandmother always liked jewelry. You know she sent me some nice things when we were married."

Then Jeanine would roll the pearl necklace around her fingers, and hold up the bright gems for her husband to see, saying: "Look! Aren't they lovely? These aren't imitation, you know."

Emil shook his head and said rather sadly, "You have extravagant[2] ideas, my dear. I'm afraid you're fond of make-believe."

Often of an evening, when they sat by the fireside, she would place on the tea table the leather box containing the "trash," as Emil called it. And then she would look at the gems as if they were the most important things in life. Often she would put a necklace around her husband's neck. Laughing heartily, she would exclaim, "How funny you look!" Then she would throw herself into his arms and kiss him sweetly.

One evening she attended the opera with some friends, and on her return she was chilled by a cold rain. The next morning she came down with cold and fever. Eight days later she died.

Emil's grief was so great that his hair turned white in one month. His heart was torn with sadness, and his mind was filled with the memory of her smile, her voice, and her beautiful charm.

II

Time, the great healer, did not lessen his sadness. Every time he thought of his loved one, his eyes filled with tears.

Strangely life became a struggle against more bad luck. Finally he was forced to take a position that paid less money. Furthermore, he began to run into debt.

One morning, finding himself without a cent in his pocket, he knew he had to sell something to raise some money. Then the thought came that he could sell some of Jeanine's jewelry. First he thought of selling the pearl necklace, which, he thought, ought to be worth six or seven francs. [3]

He put the necklace into his pocket and started out in search of a jewelry store. He entered the first one he saw, feeling a little ashamed to offer such a worthless thing for sale.

"Sir," he said to the merchant, "I would like to know what this is worth."

The man took the necklace, examined it, called his clerk
and made some quiet remarks, and then he looked at it more
carefully under a bright light.

Emil became annoyed. He was on the point of saying,

"Oh, I know it isn't worth much." Then the jeweler said, "Sir, this necklace is worth from twelve to fifteen thousand francs, but I couldn't buy it unless you tell me how you got it."

Emil opened his eyes wide. He could not believe what he had heard. Finally he stammered, "Twelve to fifteen thousand francs?"

The jeweler replied, "Well, you can try elsewhere and see if anybody will make you a better offer. Come back here if you can't do better."

Surprised beyond words, Emil took the necklace and walked outside. "The fool!" he said to himself. "Why didn't I take him at his word. He doesn't know the difference between real pearls and paste."[4]

A few minutes later he went into another store. As soon as the merchant looked at the necklace, he cried, "Ah, I remember it. It was bought here!"

Emil became worried and asked, "How much is it worth?"

"Well, I sold it for twenty thousand francs. I'm willing to take it back for eighteen thousand if you'll tell me where you got it. This is a legal formality,[5] you know."

This time Emil was greatly surprised. "Examine it well," he said. "I was afraid it was an imitation. My wife, I know, bought quite a bit of costume jewelry."

"There's no doubt that the necklace is real," the merchant said. And then he had a second thought. Why did the man act so strangely? Fearing he was dealing with a thief, he said, "Will you leave the necklace here for twenty-four hours until I have a chance to check my records. I'll give you a receipt."

"Certainly," Emil answered hastily. Then, putting the ticket into his pocket, he left the store.

He began to wander through the street, and his mind began to fill with dreadful thoughts. He tried to reason, to understand. How was it that his wife had such a costly[6] necklace? He could never have afforded its purchase. Then he thought: Was it a present from somebody? A present! A present from whom? Why was it given to her?

He stopped and remained standing in the middle of the street, as horrible thoughts ran through his mind. He broke into tears when he remembered his beautiful, sweet wife. He could not believe that she was a fickle[7] person who would invite such gifts from any other man. Then he wondered: Had she told him the truth about the necklace? Was it possible that she had been a thief?

Emil tried to dismiss from his mind the horrible thoughts that tormented him and tore at his heart.

III

The following morning he arose early to go to the office. But he had not slept much the night before, and he did not feel well. He sent a note to his employer saying that he could not come in that day. Then he remembered that he had to return to the jeweler's. He did not wish to leave the necklace with the man, so he dressed and went into the city.

It was a beautiful day. A clear blue sky smiled on the busy city. Everybody seemed happy.

Observing the people, Emil said to himself, "People who have money can forget their troubles. Oh, I wish I were rich!"

He began to feel hungry, but he had no money. His debts had a way of emptying his purse quickly. Then he remembered the necklace. Eighteen thousand francs! What a sum of money!

Finally he came to the jeweler's store. Five times he started to enter the door but fear held him back. Why . . . oh, why had he come to this?

Even the passersby[8] noted his strange behavior. Some turned to look at him, wondering what was wrong with him.

Emil was hungry, very hungry—with not a cent in his pockets. He decided quickly and entered the store.

The jeweler recognized him and came forward immediately to offer him a chair. He said, "I'm willing to pay you the price I offered if you'll sign this bill of sale[9] and tell me where you got the necklace."

"It was my wife's," Emil said. And then he added quickly, "I believe you said you had to check some kind of record. Isn't that so?"

"Oh, yes," the jeweler said, "I have done that and I remember the sale well. It was the largest sale I made the first week I opened my store. I sold the necklace to Madame Massou of St. Germain. That was almost three years ago."

"Madame Massou!" Emil exclaimed, and then he smiled broadly. "Oh, Madame Massou was Jeanine's—my wife's grandmother."

"Very good, sir," the jeweler replied. Then he went to a safe, opened it, and took out eighteen large bills. He counted them into Emil's trembling hands. Emil had never seen so much money at once in his whole life.

On the way out of the store he said to himself, "Ah, a gift from a doting[10] grandmother, of course. I wonder . . . I wonder if any more pieces of Jeanine's jewelry are real?"

• *Building Your Vocabulary*

1.	adorn	to add to the beauty of; to ornament
2.	extravagant	unreasonable; foolish
3.	francs	a type of French money
4.	paste	a lead glass used in making imitation jewelry
5.	formality	a required way of doing something
6.	costly	expensive
7.	fickle	changeable; disloyal
8.	passersby	people who walk by

9. **bill of sale**   a signed paper showing transfer of ownership
10. **doting**   foolishly fond

• *Exercises*

A. Write an expression that would complete each sentence correctly.
1. Jeanine was the daughter of a country _____.
2. Jeanine loved to adorn herself with costume _____.
3. Some of Jeanine's jewelry sparkled like real _____.
4. Emil shook his head and said rather sadly, "You have _____ ideas, my dear."
5. Emil decided to try to sell the _____ necklace.

B. Decide whether each of the following statements is true or false. Write T for *true* and F for *false*.
1. Emil Lantin had a business of his own.
2. Jeanine was beautiful and she was charming.
3. The Lantins became unhappy in their marriage.
4. Jeanine loved to attend the theater.
5. Emil told Jeanine that she should not wear imitation jewelry.
6. Emil finally had to take a position that paid less money.
7. Jeanine's grandmother lived in Paris.
8. The first merchant to whom Emil showed the pearl necklace said the gems were imitations.
9. Emil feared that his wife had been a fickle person.
10. Jeanine told her husband that her father had given her some nice things.

C. Write the letter of the definition in column II that most closely matches each expression in column I.

I. Word	II. Definition
1. doting	A. changeable; disloyal
2. francs	B. a required way of doing something
3. extravagant	C. a signed paper showing transfer of
4. formality	ownership
5. adorn	D. unreasonable; foolish
6. costly	E. a type of French money
7. paste	F. to add to the beauty of; to ornament
8. passersby	G. expensive
9. fickle	H. foolishly fond
10. bill of sale	I. a lead glass used in making imitation jewelry
	J. people who walk by

D. Write a paragraph or two on one of the following topics:

1. Tell how Emil met Jeanine and how they seemed quite happy together.
2. In what ways was Jeanine's attitude toward costume jewelry different from Emil's?
3. Discuss the reasons for Emil's becoming unhappy.
4. Describe Emil's experiences in selling the pearl necklace.

The Speckled Beauty

Ralph V. Cutlip

I

Jeanie Riley came out of the dentist's office smiling. She had had good news. The dentist had just told her that the braces on her upper front teeth could come off in six months. She walked toward home rapidly, humming quietly to herself. Her purse hung idly over her left arm and her hand clutched two books. Jeanie knew that homework that evening would be easier than usual.

Suddenly she stopped at a store window. With her right hand she swept her long blonde hair back from her forehead. Her face lighted when she saw the size ten light blue dress on a model in the window.

The blonde model smiled at Jeanie. "How beautiful!" Jeanie thought to herself, admiring the dress and the model in turn. Looking at the model more closely, Jeanie thought, "She has no freckles like me, but my hair is as pretty as hers—if not more so—and mine is real."

Then Jeanie caught a view of herself in a tall mirror in the window—and her smile faded. The image mocked her. She tried to smile again.

"Who's kidding who anyway?" she mumbled to herself. In the bright light the freckles on her cheeks and the bridge[1] of her nose looked darker than ever.

Then Jeanie's arm hung limp. She almost dropped her books and purse. Her mouth opened in dismay. The braces on her teeth helped to turn her upper lip into a snarl.[2] "Ugh!" she exclaimed. "I can't believe it. I am getting taller and uglier every day!"

Tears came to her eyes, and she turned away from the window. Her world seemed to come to an end!

With slowed steps she walked on, not stopping to look into any more store windows. Suddenly she heard faraway voices.

"Hello, Jeanie."

"Hello, Freckles."

"Hi, Beautiful!"

Jeanie came back to life.

"Hi, Beautiful." That was the voice of Tommy Benson, the flashy quarterback on the Mt. View High School junior varsity.

Somehow Jeanie managed a smile, said "Hello," and hurried on.

"Was Tommy making fun of her," she wondered, "or was he trying to be nice?"

That Tommy! He had a nice way about everything. Besides he was tall, dark, and handsome. Everybody liked him. Jeanie smiled again.

The first voice was that of Betty Coles, a sophomore like herself and her tennis partner most of the time during gym. The second voice—who could forget him? He was Mr. Snob himself, Don Parker! Well, that Don—she could think of some good names for him, and some day she would tell him—right in front of everybody!

Jeanie stopped at the corner and waited for the light to change. The street traffic was light, and though the voices were fading, she overheard Betty Coles say, "I think you have your nerve, Don Parker—calling Jeanie names like that! I think she's cute."

"I thought I was being nice," Don said. "Most of the boys call her the Speckled Beauty."

"Cut it!" Tommy said. "I agree with Betty, and I hear she's going to be the best tennis player in town. Anyway, she's got pretty eyes."

"What do you know about girls' eyes?" Betty asked.

The voices faded.

The lights at the corner changed twice, but Jeanie stood still as if she were in shock.

"Speckled Beauty? So that's what the boys were thinking! Well, maybe not Tommy." Jeanie tossed her head, pushed her hair back, and crossed the street.

II

That evening, after dinner, Jeanie took her brand new Clipper racket, went outside to the garage, and began to bounce a ball against the wooden doors.

The racket was a birthday gift from her father.

The sound of the ball thumping against the copper-coated steel strings was the sweetest music Jeanie knew. She bounced the ball from every possible angle and worked hard on her backhand and forehand. Jeanie knew she wasn't going to win any beauty contests, but she felt strange magic in her whole being every time she swung the racket. For a few seconds her cheeks warmed when she recalled Tommy's remark that afternoon: "Anyway, she's got pretty eyes."

III

During the gym period at school next day she beat Betty in a fast set—6-3.

"Gee," Betty complained, "you play as though your life depended on it. I just play for fun."

"Maybe my life does depend on it," Jeanie answered quietly.

"I don't understand," Betty said.

"It's like this," Jeanie said. "Everybody has something worthwhile—a special talent, or maybe being pretty like you."

"Thanks," Betty said, "but I still don't understand."

"Well, I don't ever expect to win any beauty contests, but my dad thinks that some day I'll be a tennis champion."

"You mean to say everybody has something going for himself," Betty said, "and all we have to do is find out what it is?"

"That's about it. Dad says it's a sort of balance in life. I hope he's right. He's always saying: 'Pretty is as pretty does,' or 'Six of one and a half dozen of the other.' I don't understand some of his expressions. I'm not always sure what he means."

"Sometimes I think our parents are way out," Betty said. "They don't seem to have the time to explain some of their ideas."

"I guess it's that generation gap talk we hear so much about. Mom said it's the same trouble people had when she was a girl. But I dig their main ideas all right. Strange how they know so much when they haven't been to school for such a long time."

"Yes, it is," Betty agreed. "Most of the things they say seem right—they're just like prophets."

"I guess we just have to have faith in ourselves and try to do what's right," Jeanie said.

IV

When school was out in June, Jeanie went to the beach with her mother for a vacation. As the dentist had promised, he removed the braces from her teeth. Jeanie was pleased with the change in her appearance. More than once she caught herself smiling in her mirror.

The Riley vacation trailer sat a half block from a public tennis court. Jeanie wished her mother could play tennis, but she seemed content just to sit on the beach during the day and read. Jeanie took a dip every morning in the ocean and then haunted[3] the tennis court like a hunter looking for game. Anybody who could swing a tennis racket was fair game.

Her toughest opponent was Carol, a red-headed girl who lived nearby. Carol was too slow to offer much competition, but she had a few trick serves—fast ones in the corners and line dusters[4] that kept Jeanie on her toes. For a while Carol was getting a few aces[5] that gave Jeanie trouble; but as Jeanie's footwork improved, she was able to return Carol's hottest serves[6] easily. Carol almost gave up playing tennis that summer, but Jeanie kept her interested by letting her win once in a while and by inviting her often to the trailer for a Coke or a hamburger.

Jeanie never knew why her father talked so much about tennis. He kept saying it was a great game and he wished he had more time to play. He talked about the great stars of yesterday. Well, he finally got around to Chris Evert, Billie Jean King, and Stan Smith, and then it was more fun to exchange ideas about players she knew.

Every weekend, when her father came down to the beach, he'd grab a tennis racket and start swinging it to show how he could serve an ace or lob[7] a ball in a smashing return. "Come on, Jeanie," he'd say, "let's play two or three sets."

Jeanie smiled, knowing that her father was as slow as a duck on dry land; but to humor him, she led the way to the tennis court. Mr. Riley lasted about one set; and unless Jeanie let him win a game, he generally came up on the short end of a 6-0 score. Then he was ready to lie in the shade of a beach umbrella.

One day he looked at Jeanie in a strange way. "My, Jeanie," he said, "the beach air and tennis are surely doing you a world of good. You're getting a nice tan, and you are filling out. Pretty soon you'll be as pretty as your mother."

Mrs. Riley smiled and Jeanie blushed.

"Filling out?" Jeanie wondered to herself. "What does he mean by that remark? Am I getting stuffed—stuffed like a hot dog?"

Then Jeanie looked at her own graceful arms and shapely legs—and smiled. She understood her father's remark. "I guess a little filling out is what I needed," she said to herself.

V

The school year was passing quickly. For several reasons the world looked brighter to Jeanie. For the first time she really liked Mt. View High, and she was making good grades. She began to have hopes of making the Honor Society, but her greatest dream was to be the district girls' singles tennis champion.

Every day after classes she had a workout with Betty. Betty was real competition, but she had big plans of her own —she was already a majorette on the drill team, and her biggest dream was that some day she would be the Homecoming Queen.

Jeanie had almost forgotten that Don Parker had called her *Freckles*. As a matter of fact, her complexion had cleared so that she was no longer conscious of her freckles. Once her mother had called them *beauty patches*. "Beauty patches? What a strange idea!" Jeanie thought.

When the day of the spring tennis matches with Central High came, Jeanie had already won the right to represent Mt. View High in the girls' singles by defeating Cora James, an outstanding black student and one of the best tennis players in school. It was Saturday and a good-sized crowd sat on the benches around the court. It was a bad day for Mt. View High. Central had already won the boys' and girls' doubles and the boys' singles. Jeanie knew she had to win or her school would be shut out completely.

Her opponent from Central High was Patsy Martino, a senior. Patsy took the first set, 6-1, in a whirl of fast action that frightened Jeanie; but she came back to take the second set, 6-2, and by this time she had begun to feel more confident.

In the third set Jeanie hoped to bring the match to an end as quickly as possible. But she was soon caught up in a volleying[8] with Patsy that brought cheers from the crowd. However, Jeanie wasn't interested in putting on a show, and it wasn't long before she had Patsy on the short end of a 5-0 score.

Jeanie needed only one more game to win the set and match, but for some unknown reason she slowed down, and then Patsy came back to win three straight games.

There were cries of dismay among the Mt. View crowd and excitement was rising. Jeanie heard cheering voices— familiar voices. One particular voice came through loud and clear, "Come on, Jeanie, you can do it!"

Jeanie heard that voice above all the others, and she heard the same kindness and sweetness she had heard once before. It was Tommy, and it sounded like "Hi, Beautiful!" And then Jeanie came to life.

It was now her service. She smiled, knowing that she had a slight advantage. She rose high on her toes and aced Patsy in the right court with a bullet drive. She followed quickly with a line duster.

"Thirty-love," the umpire called.

Patsy caught the next serve easily, and the ball hit the top of the net and rolled sideways out of reach on Jeanie's side.

Then Jeanie faulted[9] into the net twice.

"Thirty-all," the umpire said.

On Jeanie's next serve, Patsy returned the ball with a hard slam, and Jeanie missed with her backhand.

"Thirty-forty," the umpire called.

For a moment Jeanie's heart sank. The game wasn't going too well for her. It would soon be over.

Jeanie tried a bullet serve and was dismayed when Patsy returned it easily. Then began a volleying that set the crowd on edge. When Jeanie caught Patsy leaning toward the net, she popped the ball to earth over Patsy's head into the back court.

"Deuce!"[10] the umpire exclaimed.

Patsy looked surprised, and her surprise doubled when she missed Jeanie's next bullet serve by an inch.

"Point—advantage server," the umpire called.

Patsy caught the next serve. Then began another exciting volleying. Back and forth the ball swept in level flight, beautiful to watch.

"This can't go on forever," Jeanie thought to herself, and she reached high in the air and smashed the ball to earth out of Patsy's reach.

"Game . . . set . . . and match!" the umpire called. With tears in her eyes, Jeanie rushed to the net, threw her arms around Patsy, and thanked her for a beautiful game.

When Jeanie walked off the court, Tommy met her at the gate. "Hi, Beautiful!" he exclaimed. "I knew you could do it."

Jeanie blushed and said, "Thanks, Tommy. You helped."

"May I drive you home, Jeanie?"

"Well, I guess so—if you want to."

"Surely, I want to," Tommy replied. "Anyway, we have some planning to do."

"What planning?" Jeanie asked.

"The Junior-Senior Prom. You are on the committee, you know."

"No, I don't know," Jeanie said. "How come?"

"As president of the class, I appointed you."

"Well, if you say so, Tommy," Jeanie replied as she felt her heart beating in her throat.

"And something else," Tommy added quickly. "I hope you will let me take you to the Prom."

"Oh, oh," Jeanie stumbled. "That will be nice."

"I'll wait for you in the Flag Court while you go to the gym," Tommy said.

"I'll hurry!" Jeanie exclaimed as her heart began to dance happily.

• *Building Your Vocabulary*

1.	**bridge**	the upper bony part of the nose
2.	**snarl**	a curling upward of the lip to show the teeth
3.	**haunted**	visited over and over again
4.	**line dusters**	balls that hit the chalk lines but are within bounds
5.	**aces**	served balls that cannot be returned
6.	**serves**	turns at putting the ball in play
7.	**lob**	hit easily in a high curve
8.	**volleying**	hitting the ball back and forth several times before a point is scored
9.	**faulted**	failed to serve the ball in the proper place
10.	**deuce**	a tied score of three or more points for each side

• *Exercises*

A. Write the letter of the expression that best completes each of the following statements:

1. Jeanie's new tennis racket was a gift from her _____.
   a. mother   *b.* father   *c.* grandmother
2. At the beach Jeanie often played with _____.
   a. Carol   *b.* Betty   *c.* Patsy
3. Jeanie's father thought that some day Jeanie would be _____.
   a. a tennis champion
   b. an honor student
   c. the Homecoming Queen at school
4. When the spring tennis matches were held, Jeanie was a _____.
   a. freshman   *b.* senior   *c.* junior

5. Betty Coles hoped that some day she would be
   _____.

   a. a cheer leader
   b. the Homecoming Queen at school
   c. a tennis champion

   B. Decide whether each of the following statements is
true or false. Write T for *true* and F for *false.*
   1. For a while Jeanie had to wear braces on her upper
      front teeth.
   2. Tommy Benson called Jeanie "Freckles."
   3. Jeanie said, "I guess we just have to have faith in our-
      selves and try to do what's right."
   4. Jeanie was pleased with her appearance after the dentist
      had removed the braces from her teeth.
   5. Mr. Riley liked to talk about tennis.
   6. Mr. Riley played a fast tennis game.
   7. Mrs. Riley often played tennis with Jeanie.
   8. Mrs. Riley referred to Jeanie's freckles as "beauty
      patches."
   9. Central High had won most of the tennis matches
      against Mt. View High.
   10. The school principal had appointed Jeanie to the Junior-
       Senior Prom Committee.

   C. Write a paragraph or two on one of the following
topics:
   1. Tell why Jeanie was unhappy at times. How did her
      physical appearance change?
   2. Tell why Jeanie probably liked Betty Coles.
   3. Tell in what ways Mr. Riley tried to help Jeanie with
      her tennis game.
   4. Describe the kind of person Tommy Benson was. Why
      would you like to know him?

D. Write the letter of the definition in column II that most closely matches each expression in column I.

I. Word	II. Definition
1. deuce	A. hit easily in a high curve
2. lob	B. failed to serve the ball in the proper place
3. bridge	
4. faulted	C. a tied score of three or more points for each side
5. snarl	
6. volleying	D. turns at putting the ball in play
7. haunted	E. the upper bony part of the nose
8. aces	F. visited over and over again
9. serves	G. balls that hit the chalk lines but are within bounds
10. line dusters	
	H. hitting the ball back and forth several times before a point is scored
	I. served balls that cannot be returned
	J. a curling upward of the lip to show the teeth

An Occurrence
at Owl Creek Bridge

Ambrose Bierce

I

A man stood upon a railroad bridge in northern Alabama, looking down into the swift water twenty feet below. The man's hands and wrists were tied behind his back. A hangman's noose had already been placed around his neck. The rope

was tied to a stout cross-timber above his head. Some boards laid loosely on the railroad crossties[1] provided a footing for him and two private soldiers of the Yankee army, directed by a sergeant. Near one end of the bridge a captain and a lieutenant stood. The captain had ordered the execution.

At either end of the bridge a sentinel[2] stood with rifle at ready.

The railroad tracks at one end of the bridge ran off into a woodland and were lost to view. In the opposite direction the tracks led past a cut in the side of the hill. On the hill was a fort. Half way up the hill, between the bridge and the fort, stood a single company of infantry, drawn up in line. The lieutenant stood ahead of the troops, the point of his sword upon the ground, his left hand resting upon his right. Except for the men at the center of the bridge, not a man moved. The captain stood with folded arms, watching the preparations quietly, but making no sign. The execution was to be carried out according to military code.[3]

The man to be hanged was about thirty-five years of age. He was a civilian, a planter who lived in the area. His features were good—a straight nose, firm mouth, broad forehead, from which his long, dark hair was combed straight back, falling behind his ears to his collar. He had a mustache and a pointed beard.

The preparations being complete, the two private soldiers stepped aside and each drew away the plank upon which he had been standing. One plank was left. One end reached into space over the water below. On that end of the plank the condemned man stood. On the opposite end of the plank the sergeant stood. At an order from the captain, he would step aside onto a railroad tie. The trap would be sprung; and as the prisoner fell, the noose would snap his neck. Neither the prisoner's face nor his eyes had been covered. He looked for a moment at his footing. He knew then it was only a matter of moments. A piece of dancing driftwood caught his attention, and his eyes followed it as it floated downstream. Down the stream! Downstream lay his plantation, and he closed his eyes to fix his last thoughts upon his wife and children. The water was touched by the gold of the morning sun. How peaceful and beautiful it looked to him!

Then the man became conscious of a strange noise that disturbed the thoughts of his loved ones. The repeated strokes sounded like a blacksmith's hammer upon an anvil.[4] At first he thought it was a death knell,[5] but the sounds came too fast. They hurt his ears like the blow of a knife, and he feared he would cry out. What he heard was the ticking of his watch.

He unclosed his eyes and saw again the water below him. "If I could free my hands," he thought, "I might throw off the noose and jump into the water and swim to the bank, take to the woods, and make my way home—home to my wife and my little ones." For a moment the man smiled at the thought.

II

The man's name was Peyton Farquhar. He was a well-to-do planter of an old and highly respected Alabama family. For reasons of health and family he was not able to fight for his beloved South. Meanwhile he did what he could to aid the Confederate army in protecting the homeland from the Northern invader.

One evening while Farquhar and his wife were sitting on a bench near the entrance to his grounds, a gray-clad soldier rode up to the gate and asked for a drink of water. Mrs. Farquhar brought the water. Meanwhile her husband asked for news from the front.

"The Yanks are repairing the railroads," the man said, "and they are getting ready for another advance. They have reached the Owl Creek Bridge, put it in order, and have built a fort on the north side of the creek. The commander has issued an order, which is posted everywhere, saying that any civilian caught interfering with the railroad, its bridges, tunnels, or the trains, will be hanged. I saw the order."

"How far is it to the bridge?" Farquhar asked.

"About thirty miles."

"Is there a Union force beyond this side of the bridge?"

"No. The Yanks are not quite ready to advance."

The next day, shortly after dark, Farquhar was caught at the southern end of the bridge. He had already piled a great amount of loose wood and tree limbs against the wooden trestle[6] and had just set the pile afire when he was surprised in the act by a Federal sentinel.

III

Peyton Farquhar smiled again. Within the few seconds that remained before the trap was to be sprung, his imagination, rejecting the idea of death, became excited to an extreme degree. His great desire to hold on to life caused images of escape to flood his mind.

First, it was easy to untie the cords that bound his wrists. All he had to do was pull his hands apart, and then raise a hand to remove the noose about his neck. Quickly he dived into the cool waters below his feet. When he rose to the surface, his lungs were bursting for the need of air. He felt his head come up, and his lungs sucked in the air. He was now physically alert, and he swam away from the bridge.

He had come to the surface facing downstream. In a moment he turned from side to side. Now he saw the bridge, the hillside, and the fort. The soldiers were shouting and pointing at him. The captain had drawn his pistol but did not fire.

Suddenly he heard a sharp report,[7] and something struck

the water within a few inches of his head. He heard a second report, and he saw one of the sentinels with his rifle at his shoulder, pointed in his direction.

Farquhar swam away as fast as he could. He heard a loud, clear voice. It was the voice of the lieutenant giving an order: "Attention, company! Ready! . . . Aim! . . . Fire!"

Farquhar dived—dived as deeply as he could. The water roared in his ears, yet he heard the thunder of the volley, [8] and he was sure he heard the bullets striking the water.

As he rose to the surface, gasping for breath, he saw that he was farther down the stream—nearer to safety. The soldiers began to reload. He saw the rifles flashing in the sunlight. This time he knew the soldiers would be firing at will. He would not likely be able to escape all the flying bullets.

Suddenly a rising sheet of water curved over him, fell down behind him, and blinded him. A cannon at the fort was taking a hand in the game. As he shook the water from his head, he heard the cannonball go crashing into the tree branches along the creek.

"They will do that again," he thought. "This is the end."

Suddenly he found himself caught in a swift current of water. And the next minute he lay against the river bank, gasping for breath. He rose to his feet, staggered out of the water, and crawled into the forest. Then he heard the cannon again. It was a farewell shot.

All day he traveled through the forest, setting his course by the sun. He had never known that he lived so close to so much wild country.

By nightfall, tired and hungry, he found the road he knew so well. At last—at last he would be home with his wife and family!

Now he stands at the gate of his home. All is as he had left it the day before, and all is bright and beautiful—even in the dimming twilight. As he pushes open the gate and passes up the wide white walk, he sees his wife, beautiful and neat, coming down the veranda[9] stairs to meet him. At the bottom of the stairs, she stands, smiling in her great joy at seeing him. Ah, how beautiful she is! He springs forward with open arms.

IV

As he was about to clasp her into his arms, the captain spoke and the lieutenant raised his sword. The sergeant stepped off his end of the board.

The trap had been sprung. The man felt a stunning[10] blow upon the back of his neck. A blinding white flash blazed about him with a sound like the shock of a cannon. Then all is darkness and silence!

Peyton Farquhar was dead. His body swung gently from side to side beneath the timbers of Owl Creek Bridge.

• Building Your Vocabulary

1.	crossties	wooden crosspieces to which railroad rails are fastened
2.	sentinel	a guard
3.	code	rules; regulations
4.	anvil	a block of iron on which metal is shaped by hammering
5.	knell	the sound of a bell rung for a death, funeral, or disaster
6.	trestle	a framework supporting a bridge
7.	report	an explosive noise
8.	volley	several shots fired at the same time
9.	veranda	a long porch
10.	stunning	able to numb or make dizzy

• *Exercises*

A. Write a short answer for each of the following questions:
1. In what state did this story take place?
2. What was Peyton Farquhar's occupation?
3. When the gray-clad soldier came to the plantation, he asked for a drink of water. Who brought the water to him?
4. Farquhar heard a noise that sounded like a blacksmith's hammer upon an anvil. What was it that made the noise?
5. On the bridge, at the time of the execution, Farquhar stood on one end of a plank. Who stood on the other end?

B. Decide whether each of the following statements is true or false. Write T for *true* and F for *false*.
1. Owl Creek Bridge was held by Yankee soldiers.
2. The Yankees had built a fort underneath the bridge.
3. Peyton Farquhar was about nineteen years old.
4. Farquhar was a soldier in the Confederate army.
5. The Yankees had not advanced beyond Owl Creek Bridge.
6. Farquhar was caught when he tried to burn the bridge.
7. The Yankees had posted a notice saying that any civilian caught interfering with the railroad, its bridges, tunnels, or the trains, would be hanged.
8. The bridge was about ten miles from Farquhar's home.
9. The execution had been ordered by the captain.
10. Farquhar escaped hanging by jumping into the water and swimming away.

C. Write the letter of the definition in column II that most closely matches each word in column I.

I. Word	II. Definition

1. stunning   A. an explosive noise
2. crossties   B. a framework supporting a bridge
3. sentinel   C. a long porch
4. anvil   D. the sound of a bell rung for a
5. trestle   death, funeral, or disaster
6. code   E. a block of iron on which metal is
7. knell   shaped by hammering
8. veranda   F. wooden crosspieces to which rail-
9. volley   road rails are fastened
10. report   G. a guard

                      H. able to numb or make dizzy

                      I. rules; regulations

                      J. several shots fired at the same time

D. Write a paragraph or two on one of the following topics:

1. Tell who Peyton Farquhar was and how he tried to slow down the Yankee advance.
2. Describe the preparations the Yankees made to hang Farquhar.
3. Describe the escape Farquhar imagined.
4. Imagine that Farquhar had been able to burn down the bridge. Tell what happened afterward.

The Servant

S. T. Semonov

I

Gerasim looked at the old beggar sadly, and he was reminded of his own problem in finding work in the big city. The beggar stood in front of a bake shop. He leaned on a cane, and his long, gray beard hid his thin face and the hunger in his eyes. Gerasim felt the small coin he kept in an inside pocket. It was his last bit of money.

"Here, Dad," he said. "Take this and buy yourself some bread."

The old man looked up slowly, not believing that he had heard correctly.

Gerasim pushed the coin into the old man's bony hand and turned away.

"Thank you, my son," the beggar said, "and may God bless you."

Gerasim had returned to Moscow just before Christmas. It was the hardest time of the year to find work. For three weeks he had walked about the streets looking for a job. While he was in the city, he had stayed with friends and relatives. Although he had not known any great want, he felt unhappy in not being able to earn his own food and lodging.[1] He had worked at all kinds of jobs—as a bottle washer in a dairy, as a clerk with a merchant, and as a house servant. He had gone back to his home village several weeks earlier, thinking he would be called up for military duty. However, he was not called and he had returned to the city.

Every day it was getting more difficult for him to be tramping the streets in idleness.[2] He had gone to all the stores and to all the shops, looking in vain for some kind of employment. He was at a loss, not knowing what to do. Sometimes he would go a whole day without eating rather than spend his last cent.

II

One day he went to see his friend Igor, who lived in the suburbs[3] of the city. The man was a coachman[4] to a merchant by the name of Sharov, in whose services he had been for many years. The merchant had great trust in Igor. It was Igor's glib[5] tongue that got him so much favor with his master. He told on all the other servants, and Sharov liked that.

When Gerasim went to Igor's house, the coachman greeted him kindly and offered him tea and food, and asked him how he was doing.

"Very badly," Gerasim said. "I've been looking for work more than three weeks now."

"Did you ask your old employer to take you back?" Igor asked.

"I did."

"He wouldn't take you again?"

"No. The position was already filled when I went back."

"Is that so? Well, that's the way with you young fellows. You don't work too well on the job and you muddle[6] things up so that you are no longer wanted. If you worked well, your masters would think better of you, and you would find it less difficult to get your job back or even to find a new one."

"Maybe I've made a few mistakes," Gerasim replied. "I don't think employers care much what happens to you if you have to leave their service."

"What's the use of wasting words on you. If for some reason or other I should ever have to leave this place and go home, Mr. Sharov would take me back when I returned, and he would be glad to."

Gerasim felt gloomy. He saw that his friend was boasting,[7] and he said, "I know, Igor, if you were a poor worker, your employer would not have kept you all these years."

Igor smiled. He liked the praise. "That's it," he said. "If you were to live and work as I do, you wouldn't be out of work so long."

Gerasim did not know what to say.

At that moment Igor was called away. "Wait here," he said, "I'll be right back."

III

Igor came back and said that inside of half an hour he had to drive his master into town. Then he lighted his pipe and spoke to Gerasim.

"Listen," he said, "if you want, I'll ask my master to take you on as a servant here."

"Does he need a man?" Gerasim asked.

"We have one, but he's not much good. He's getting

old, and it's very hard for him to do the work needed of him."

"Oh, if you can, please say a word for me. I can't stand to be without work a day longer."

"All right," Igor replied. "Come again tomorrow, and in the meantime I shall see what I can do."

Gerasim left, and Igor went to get the horses and sleigh. Then he put on his coachman's hat and drove up to the front door. Mr. Sharov came out and seated himself in the sleigh and rode into town to take care of some business.

On the way back Igor saw that his master was in a good humor, and he said to him, "Sir, I have a favor to ask of you."

"Yes, what is it?"

"There's a young man here from my village, a good boy. He's looking for work. Can you take him?"

"What do I want him for?"

"Use him as a helper around the place."

"How about the old man—Polik?"

"What good is he? It's about time you let him go, anyway."

"That wouldn't be fair," Sharov replied. "He's been here many years. I cannot let him go without a good reason."

"Well, he hasn't worked for nothing all these years," Igor said. "Certainly he has saved some money for his old age."

"Saved up? How could he? He's not alone in the world. He has a wife to support."

"His wife earns money, too. She does housecleaning," Igor said.

"A lot that would be!" Sharov exclaimed. "Not enough for bread."

"Why should you care for Polik and his wife?" Igor argued. "He's a poor worker. Why should you throw away your money on him? He never shovels the snow away on time, and he never does anything right. And when it comes his turn to be night watchman, he slips away ten times a night. It's too cold for him. You'll see, some day, because of him, you'll have trouble."

"Still it's pretty rough," Sharov replied. "He's been here fifteen years. And to let him go in his old age would be a sin."

"He won't starve," Igor said. "He can always go to the poorhouse—if he needs to. Anyway, it would be quieter and easier than trying to work here."

Sharov thought a moment. "All right," he said. "Bring your friend and I'll see what I can do."

"Thank you," Igor said. "He's a good worker and he'll serve you well. His former master would have kept him if he had not had to report for military duty."

IV

The next morning when Gerasim came to see Igor, he asked, "Well, could you do anything for me?"

"Yes, perhaps. First, let's have some tea and we'll go to see my master."

Gerasim was so excited that he had no interest in the tea. But, being polite to Igor, he gulped down two cupfuls, and then they went to see Sharov.

Sharov asked Gerasim where he had worked before and what kind of work he had done. Then he told him to come back the next day and be ready to work.

Gerasim was stunned[8] by his sudden good luck. Then he went back to the coachman's room with Igor.

"Well, my lad," Igor said, "see to it that you do your work well. You know what masters are like. If you go wrong once, they'll be at you forever with their fault-finding."

When Gerasim left, he went through the yard. He had to pass the rooms where old Polik and his wife lived. He knew that soon the rooms would be his place to live. He heard two people talking. One, a woman, was weeping.

"What will we do now?" she cried.

"I don't know, I don't know," old Polik replied. "Go begging on the streets, I suppose."

"Heaven help us!" the poor woman exclaimed.

"That's all we can do. There's nothing else left. Oh, we poor people work from morning until night, day after day; and when we get old, that's the end of the road. What will we do? What will we do?"

"Why did the master let you go?" the woman asked.

"The master's not so much to blame," Polik said. "It's Igor. He wants his friend to work in my place. It doesn't seem fair when we have been here so long and done our work well."

"Yes, he's a serpent, and he knows how to talk fast and lie. I think we should go to the master and tell him how Igor steals his fodder⁹ and sells it and puts the money into his own pocket. I'll put it all down in writing. We know the truth about Igor."

"Don't!" Polik said. "Don't sin!"

"Sin? Is it a sin to tell the truth?" the woman said as she began to cry.

Gerasim heard all this and it stabbed him like a knife. He realized for the first time how difficult it would be for the old people if he took Polik's place. Then he remembered the old beggar he had met one day on the street. A strange feeling overcame him.

He stood there a long time, feeling sad, and lost in thought. Then he turned and walked back to the coachman's room, where Igor was doing some work.

"Well, did you forget something?" Igor asked.

"No," Gerasim replied. "I've come to tell you something. Thank you for trying to help me. I appreciate your efforts—the trouble you took for me—but I cannot take the job."

"What! What does that mean?" Igor asked.

"Nothing. I don't want the place.[10] I'll look for something else. I'll find a job!"

Igor flew into a rage. "Did you mean to make a fool of me?" he shouted. "You came here crying for work. Now you've changed your mind, and you have made me look stupid!"

Gerasim had nothing else to say in reply. He reddened and lowered his eyes. Then he picked up his cap and left the coachman's room.

As he walked toward the house, he met Sharov in the yard.

For some reason Sharov was serious and unsmiling. "Be here tomorrow at seven," he said. "I want you to help the Poliks pack their things."

Gerasim removed his cap and said, "Sir, I cannot take the job. I came to tell you."

"Why . . . why this sudden change of mind?" Sharov asked somewhat surprised.

"I cannot take the old man's position. He needs the work more than I do. I appreciate the offer."

Sharov looked at Gerasim thoughtfully for a moment and then said, "You are right. I don't think the Poliks should go to the poorhouse."

"I'll find a job somewhere," Gerasim said.

"I am sure you will," Sharov said. "I am sure you will! I'll go now and tell the Poliks that they may stay. Good luck, young man. Let me know if I can ever help you."

Gerasim crossed the yard rapidly and went out the gate and walked down the street, feeling happy and lighthearted.

• *Building Your Vocabulary*

1. **lodging**   a sleeping place
2. **idleness**   spending time doing nothing
3. **suburbs**   outlying parts of a city
4. **coachman**   a driver of a horse-drawn carriage
5. **glib**   speaking with careless ease
6. **muddle**   to make a mess of
7. **boasting**   bragging about oneself
8. **stunned**   dazed; astonished
9. **fodder**   coarse feed for cattle; generally corn stalks and hay
10. **place**   job; position

• *Exercises*

A. Write an expression that would complete each sentence correctly.
1. Gerasim returned to Moscow just before _____.
2. Gerasim's friend was _____, a coachman for Mr. Sharov.
3. Mr. Sharov came out and seated himself in the _____ and rode into town to take care of some business.
4. Sharov asked _____ where he had worked before and what kind of work he had done.
5. "Yes, he's a _____, and he knows how to talk fast and lie," Polik's wife said.

B. Decide whether each of the following statements is true or false. Write T for *true* and F for *false*.
1. Gerasim had gone back to his home village, thinking he would be called up for military duty.

2. The Christmas season was the hardest time to find work.
3. Sometimes Gerasim went a whole day without having anything to eat.
4. Igor drove his master to town in a wagon.
5. From the beginning Sharov was pleased with the idea of getting rid of old Polik.
6. Old Polik's wife earned a small amount of money at housecleaning.
7. Igor said that old Polik and his wife could go to the poorhouse.
8. Old Polik and his wife knew that Igor stole from his master.
9. When Gerasim realized how poor Polik and his wife were, he refused to take the job.
10. Igor was pleased to hear that Gerasim did not take the job.

C. Write the letter of the definition in column II that most closely matches each word in column I.

I. Word	II. Definition
1. fodder	A. a sleeping place
2. suburbs	B. to make a mess of
3. boasting	C. dazed; astonished
4. muddle	D. speaking with careless ease
5. place	E. a driver of a horse-drawn carriage
6. coachman	F. coarse feed for cattle; generally corn stalks or hay
7. glib	
8. idleness	G. spending time doing nothing
9. stunned	H. bragging about oneself
10. lodging	I. job; position
	J. outlying parts of a city

D. Write a paragraph or two on one of the following topics:

1. Tell why Gerasim was looking for work.
2. Tell how Igor tried to help Gerasim. What kind of person was Igor? Why did he scold Gerasim?
3. Tell why Gerasim refused the job that was offered him. Do you think his meeting the old beggar in the earlier part of the story had anything to do with his decision?
4. Perhaps you would like to tell about some of your experiences in looking for work.

Love of Life

Jack London

The man had fallen into the creek and had sprained his ankle.

He called to his friend: "I say, Bill, wait there. I've sprained my ankle."

There was no answer. Bill had disappeared in the damp fog. Although it was still August, the Canadian wilderness lay cold and lonely in the weak light of the afternoon sun. Everywhere was the dull skyline. The hills were all low-lying. There were no trees. There was nothing but desolation[1] that sent fear into the man's heart.

"Bill!" he called again. "Bill!" There was no answer.

The man rose to his feet, shaking as if he had a fever. He fought against the fear in his heart. He found his gun where he had dropped it in the water. Then he continued his way slowly. The gun was now useless, for he had no ammunition for it, but he did not leave it.

He shifted his pack to his left shoulder so as to favor

his right ankle and hurried to the top of a hill. From there he saw a broad valley, empty of life.

The bottom of the valley was soft and swampy. He pushed on, trying to follow the tracks of his companion.

Though he was now alone, he was not lost. Farther along he knew where to find the trail. He would follow it until it came to the river, where they had left their canoe, weighted down with rocks. Under the canoe was a cache[2] of ammunition for his empty gun, fishhooks and lines, and a small net. He would also find some flour, bacon, and beans—not much, for they had taken most of their food with them on their trip into the north country looking for gold.

He knew Bill would wait for him there; then they would paddle down the river to a Hudson Bay Company post, where there would be warm shelter and plenty of food.

These were the thoughts of the man as he limped along the trail. Then he began to think that perhaps Bill had deserted him. The man had not eaten for two days, and now was the added fear of starvation. He had stopped a few times to eat some wild berries, but they were mostly seeds and bitter. His hunger increased by the hour.

Already the sun had slipped beyond the horizon.[3] Suddenly he struck his toe on a rocky ledge and fell. He lay still for some time without movement. Then he slipped out of his pack straps and dragged himself to a sitting position. It was not yet dark, and in the lingering twilight he gathered some moss. When he had a good-sized pile, he built a fire and set a small pail of water over the fire to boil.

He unwrapped his pack, and the first thing he did was to count his matches. There were sixty-seven. He counted them three times to make sure. He divided them into three small packs, wrapping them in oil paper, putting one bunch in his empty tobacco pouch, another bunch in the inside band of his hat, and the third bunch under his shirt on his chest.

He was afraid that if he fell into the water again, all of his matches would become wet and useless.

He dried his footgear by the fire. The wet moccasins had been cut to pieces. The socks were worn through in places, and his ankle had swollen to the size of his knee. He tore a long strip from one of his blankets and bound the ankle tightly. He tore other strips and bound them about his feet for footwear. He was cold, and he knew that there would soon be the danger of snow and frost. After the water heated, he drank some of it; then he wound his watch, and crawled between his blankets. He slept like a dead man.

At six o'clock he awoke, lying on his back. He gazed straight up into the gray sky and knew that he was hungry. As he rolled over on his elbow, he heard a loud snort and saw a caribou[4] looking at him strangely. The animal was not more than fifty feet away, and instantly the man had thoughts of a caribou steak frying over a fire. He reached for his empty gun, aimed, and pulled the trigger. The animal snorted at the click of the empty gun and ran away.

The man cursed and groaned aloud as he dragged himself to his feet. Slowly he rolled his pack together. He looked at the moose-hide bag that he carried in his pack. It was extra weight, and he began to wonder what value its contents had now. However, he rolled it together with his pack and started out.

The pain in his ankle was terrific, but it was no worse than that in his empty stomach. The hunger had become frightful. In a little while he came upon a valley where some birds rose on whirring[5] wings. "Ker . . . ker . . . ker," they cried as they flew away. He threw stones but he could not hit a one. He placed his pack on the ground and began to stalk[6] the birds like a cat.

The sharp rocks cut through his pants legs till his knees were scratched and bleeding, but he was not aware of his hurts as his hunger was so great. He cursed the birds and mocked[7] them with their own cry.

As the day wore on, he came into a valley where game was more plentiful. A herd of twenty caribou passed by within rifle range. He felt like running after them, but he knew such an effort would be senseless. Once he saw a fox with a bird in its mouth. He called loudly, hoping to frighten the fox into dropping the bird; but the fox, leaping away in fright, did not drop the bird.

He was weary and often wished to rest—to lie down and sleep, but he was driven on by his hunger. He searched little ponds for frogs and dug up the earth with his finger nails for worms, though he knew that neither frogs nor worms lived that far north.

In one area he walked along a creek, looking for fish. In a pool he found a small one. He dipped his arm into the water up to his shoulder, but the fish got away. Then he reached for it with both hands, stirring up the mud at the bottom. In his excitement he fell in, wetting himself to the waist. Since he could no longer see the fish, he had to wait until the water cleared.

When he tried again, the water became muddy. Then he took his tin pail and began to bail[8] the pool. He bailed wildly at first, and some of the water ran back into the pool. Then he worked more carefully, though his heart was pounding in his chest and his hands were shaking. At the end of half an hour the pool was nearly dry. But there was no fish. It had escaped between the rocks into a larger pool.

Defeated in his effort, the man sat down upon the wet earth. At first he cried softly to himself. Then he cried loudly in his hopeless condition.

He built a fire and warmed himself and drank some hot water. His blankets were wet and cold, and his ankle was still painful, but his worst suffering came from his hunger.

He tried to sleep, but he dreamed of food and many good things to eat.

He awoke cold and sick. There was no sun. The air about him grew white while he made a fire and boiled some water. It was wet snow, half rain, and the flakes melted quickly and put out his fire.

By this time he had become hunger-mad. He felt through the snow and pulled up some grass roots. He chewed the roots but they were tasteless or bitter.

He had no fire that night because he couldn't find any dry wood, so he crawled under his blanket to sleep the broken sleep of hunger. The snow turned into a cold rain. He felt it on his face during the night.

Late the next morning the sun broke through the gray mist. Then the man realized he was lost. He turned northward to correct his course, hoping to find the river and the canoe. Then he wondered what had happened to Bill.

Though his hunger pains were no worse, he realized he was getting weaker. He had to stop frequently to rest. His tongue felt dry and large, and his mouth had a bitter taste. His heart gave him a great deal of trouble. He could feel its thump, thump, thump; and the painful beats choked him and made him feel faint.

In the middle of the day he caught two small fish in a pool by using his pail. He ate the fish raw, but the hunger pain was now dull and lifeless. His stomach had gone to sleep.

In the morning he caught three more small fish, eating two of them and saving one for his breakfast.

Another night passed. In the morning he tied more strips of the blanket around his feet, and then he untied the string of the moose-hide pouch. From its open mouth poured a yellow stream of coarse gold dust and nuggets. He knew he must lighten his load. He hardly had the strength to carry the last remaining blanket. He roughly divided the gold into halves. He poured half of the gold into a piece of blanket and rolled it into a small package, which he hid in a rock ledge.

Then he walked on, barely able to place one foot ahead of the other.

He faced another day of cold fog. Half of his last blanket had gone to wrap his feet. He was now too weak to carry his small pack. Again he divided the gold, this time by spilling half of it on the ground. In the afternoon he threw the rest of it away. There remained only the half blanket, the tin pail, his knife, and the rifle.

He pushed on for an hour before he fell into a faint. Aroused by a noise, he could not believe his eyes. Before him stood a horse. A horse! Rubbing his eyes, he suddenly realized he was looking at a great brown bear.

The man brought his gun half way to his shoulder before he remembered it was not loaded. He lowered it and drew his hunting knife, wondering if the bear would attack. The man drew himself up to his full height, stared at the bear and waited. The bear advanced a few steps and then stopped. The man knew if he ran, the bear would run after him. With all his might the man swung the knife and growled like an animal. The bear did not understand the mysterious creature and walked away.

The man pulled himself together and went on, afraid now in a new way. There were wolves. Now and again the wolves, in packs of two and three, crossed his path. They stayed clear of the man, for it was easier to hunt the caribou.

In the late afternoon he came upon the bones of a caribou calf. He sat on the moss and gathered the bones into a heap, and then he chewed them with his bare teeth, trying to get a mouthful of the raw meat. Then he pounded the bones between rocks, beating them into a pulp⁹ and swallowed it. In his haste he almost broke some of his fingers, yet he did not mind the hurt.

Then came frightful days of snow and rain. The will to

live carried him on. It was the life in him, unwilling to die, that drove him on. By this time he had become numb to pain. Half alive, he walked, he stumbled, he crawled until he came to a river. His dull senses told him it was not the same river where he and Bill had left their canoe. He followed the course of the river downstream. He didn't know where he was—it didn't matter much anyway. But he still had the will to live, and he pushed on.

He awoke one morning, lying on his back on a rocky ledge. In a painful effort, he rolled over on his side. Below him he could see that the river flowed out to the sea. He was not excited about that fact, and then he saw something that he was sure was a trick of the mind. Maybe, after all, it was a dream—a ship lying at anchor. He closed his eyes and then opened them. The ship was still there. The man could not believe it.

Then the man heard a noise behind him—a half-choking gasp or cough. He could see nothing near at hand. Again came the strange noises, and outlined against the rocks twenty feet away was the gray head of a wolf. The animal had bloodshot eyes. It seemed sick. It was no longer able to hunt with the packs. It even feared its own kind, but now it stalked the man, waiting for him to die.

The man looked again toward the sea. He decided the ship was real. It was at least five miles away, but the man had the will to live. He no longer felt the hunger. His last blanket was gone, and he had lost the rifle.

Though extremely weak, he was calm. He ripped off his pants legs to the knees and bound them to his feet. His movements were slow, but he was determined. He still had some matches and the tin pail. He warmed some water and drank it. Now he felt slightly better, and he was able to stand. He walked toward the ship until his weakness overcame him. Then he crawled on all fours like an animal.

In the late afternoon he saw an empty moose-hide sack

like his. He recognized it and knew it was Bill's. A hundred yards farther were the bones of a human skeleton. The man did not need to guess. Bill had almost made it!

Finally the man lay quiet in sleep. Two or three times during the night the sick wolf had come close to the man, bared its teeth, and sniffed in hunger, but the man flung his arms out and scared the wolf away.

The first rays of daylight brought the man to life. He was no longer able to stand, so he began to crawl toward the ship. He could see it now—lying beyond the breakers.[10] His knees and arms were raw and bleeding, but the man kept moving, a foot at a time, until he reached the beach, where he lay quietly—unable to move a foot farther. He dreamed of food, clean clothing, and warm sunshine, and then he began to crawl again.

The ship was the *Bedford*, once a whaling vessel. On board were the members of a scientific expedition. Some of the members saw a strange object crawling along the beach toward the water. They were unable to identify the object, and being scientific men, they climbed into a ship's boat and went ashore to see. And they saw something that was hardly alive and could hardly be called a human being. It moved along the ground like a worm and made headway at perhaps twenty feet an hour.

The man was brought aboard the *Bedford*, given food, and cared for by a doctor.

In a few days he was able to sit up in his bunk. With tears streaming down his cheeks, he told how he had almost lost his life in the wilds. Then he began to talk strangely of his family in sunny southern California, and of a home among the orange trees and the flowers.

• *Building Your Vocabulary*

1.	**desolation**	gloominess; loneliness
2.	**cache**	a hidden supply
3.	**horizon**	the line where the earth meets the sky; as far as one can see
4.	**caribou**	a large reindeer found in Canada
5.	**whirring**	moving rapidly with a buzzing sound
6.	**stalk**	to hunt in a sly way
7.	**mocked**	made fun of
8.	**bail**	to dip and throw out water with a bucket
9.	**pulp**	a soft mass of material
10.	**breakers**	waves breaking into foam against the shore

• *Exercises*

A. Write the letter of the expression that best completes each of the following statements:

1. This story takes place in _____.
   a. Alaska   *b*. Canada   *c*. Montana
2. When the man fell into the creek, he sprained his _____.
   a. knee   *b*. elbow   *c*. ankle
3. The man did not have _____.
   a. ammunition   *b*. a knife   *c*. a gun
4. The man's worst suffering came from _____.
   a. the cold rain
   b. a sprained ankle
   c. hunger
5. The most useless thing the man carried was a _____.
   a. knife   *b*. sack of gold   *c*. tin pail

B. Write the letter of the definition in column II that most closely matches each word in column I.

I. Word	II. Definition
1. breakers	A. to dip and throw out water with a bucket
2. cache	
3. caribou	B. a soft mass of material
4. stalk	C. made fun of
5. bail	D. moving rapidly with a buzzing sound
6. desolation	
7. horizon	E. to hunt in a sly way
8. mocked	F. the line where the earth meets the sky; as far as the eye can see
9. pulp	
10. whirring	G. gloominess; loneliness
	H. a hidden supply
	I. waves breaking into foam against the shore
	J. a large reindeer found in Canada

C. Decide whether each of the following statements is true or false. Write T for *true* and F for *false.*

1. The man and his friend Bill had gone into the north country to look for gold.
2. On the return trip, each man carried a small sack of gold.
3. The men were headed back to the Hudson Bay Company post.
4. The man had a small amount of food with him.
5. The man lost all his matches when he fell into the creek.
6. The man's moccasins had been cut to pieces.
7. There was plenty of wild game in the country.
8. The pack of wolves stayed clear of the man, for it was easier for them to hunt the caribou.

9. A sick gray wolf followed the man, waiting for him to die.
10. Bill, the man's partner, got back safely.

D. Write a paragraph or two on one of the following topics:

1. Try to imagine why Bill left his friend, and tell what happened to him.
2. Tell how the man looked for food. What were some of the things he ate?
3. Tell about the experiences the man had with different wild animals.
4. Try to imagine that the man found the canoe and the cache of food and ammunition. Tell what he did then.

The Ransom
of Red Chief

O. Henry

Bill and I had teamed together a long time, living more or less by our wits. He and I together had saved up about six hundred dollars. We needed two thousand more for a real estate deal we had cooked up. The easiest way to get the money, we thought, was to try kidnapping. We knew there were many risks, but we decided to go ahead anyway, not thinking of the penalty we might have to pay.

We selected Summit, Alabama, as the place to try our luck. Our victim was Johnny Dorset, the son of the town banker. Johnny was a freckled-faced youngster of ten, red-haired and full of life. But how did we know he was the town's Little Devil!

Well, our plan was this: About two miles from town there was a little mountain covered with cedar trees. Near the top of the mountain was a cave. There we stored our provisions[1] and waited for our opportunity.

One evening after sundown, we drove in a buggy[2] past the Dorset house. The kid was in the street, throwing rocks at a kitten on a fence.

"Hey, little boy!" Bill called, "would you like to have a bag of candy and a nice ride?"

A piece of brick caught Bill above his right eye.

"That will cost the old man an extra five hundred," Bill said, climbing down.

That boy put up a bit of a fight. But at last we got him into the buggy, and we drove away to the cave. After dark I took the buggy back to the stable, where I had rented it.

When I got back, Bill had nursed his wounds, including the ones on his shins, where the kid had kicked him.

"He's all right now," Bill said. "We're playing Indian. We're making Buffalo Bill's show look like a kid circus. I'm Old Hank, the Trapper. He's Red Chief. He's going to scalp me or burn me at the stake. He hasn't made up his mind yet. I'm afraid he is going to do both."

Yes, sir, the boy was having the time of his life playing Indian. He immediately christened[3] me Snake Eye, and promised to burn me at the stake as soon as his braves returned from the warpath.

Then we had supper. The kid filled his mouth with bacon, bread, and gravy, and began to talk.

"I like playing Indian just fine," he said. "I never camped out before. I'm never going home. No—never, never. I hate school. I want some more bacon. I have five puppies at home. My father has lots of money. Do the trees make the wind blow? Are the stars hot? I don't like girls. Why are oranges round? Amos Murray has six toes. Why do my freckles stay on after I wash my face?"

Every few minutes he picked up his stick rifle, let out a war whoop, and started looking around the cave for palefaces. That boy had Bill scared to death from the start.

"Red Chief," I said to the kid, "would you like to go home?"

"Aw, what for?" he said. "I don't have any fun at home. I like to camp out. You won't take me home again, Snake Eye, will you?"

"Not right away," I said. "We'll stay here in the cave awhile."

"Aw right," he said. "That'll be fine. I never had such fun in all my life."

That night we spread our blankets on the ground. Red Chief slept between us. We weren't afraid he'd run away, but we thought we had a better chance of saving our own lives that way.

Just at daybreak I was awakened by screams from Bill. I jumped up to see what was the matter. Red Chief was sitting on Bill's chest, his hand twined[4] in Bill's hair. In the other hand he had our kitchen knife and was trying to take Bill's scalp.

I got the knife from Red Chief and made him lie down again. Poor Bill—his spirit was broken. He never slept any more as long as the kid was with us. I lit my pipe and leaned against a rock. I just remembered that Red Chief had said I was to be burned at the stake at sunrise.

"Why are you getting up so soon?" Bill asked.

"Me?" I said. "Oh, I got a pain in my shoulder. I can't sleep any more."

"Liar!" Bill said. "You're afraid. The kid said he was going to burn you at the stake at sunrise. He'll do it too if he can find a match. Do you think anybody will pay money to get that little imp[5] back?"

"Sure," I said. "A rowdy kid like that is just the kind that parents dote[6] on. Now you and Red Chief cook some breakfast. I'll go into town and look around a little. We'd better arrange the ransom right away."

"Ransom?" Bill howled. "Take him with you. Turn him loose! Get rid of him. We'd better hide from him."

The town was perfectly quiet. There was no sign of alarm. No peace officers ran around looking for a lost kid. There were no people dredging[7] the river or looking through the swamps for a lost boy. As a matter of fact, the town was at peace.

When I got back to the cave, I found Bill almost in tears.

"He put a red-hot boiled potato down my back," he explained.

After breakfast the kid took a slingshot out of his pocket. He picked up a good-sized piece of gravel and started to wind up. I dodged, but poor Bill got it in the back of his neck.

I caught the boy and shook him until his freckles rattled.

"If you don't behave," I said, "I'll take you straight home. Now are you going to be good?"

"I was only funning," the kid said. "If you promise not to take me home, I'll be nice to Old Hank."

"We'll have to write a ransom note," I said to Bill. "You entertain him while I deliver the note."

"His folks will never pay two thousand dollars for him," Bill said. "It ain't human for anybody in his right mind to pay that much money for that chunk of wildcat. You'd better take a chance at fifteen hundred."

So, to relieve Bill, we worded a letter to Mr. Dorset:

To: Mr. Ebenezer Dorset

Sir, we have your boy. We demand fifteen hundred dollars in small bills for his return. The money is to be brought by a lone messenger at midnight. After crossing the Rock Creek bridge, he will see three poplar trees. Opposite the third tree is a fence post. At the base of the post will be a cardboard box. He must leave the money in the box.

If you pay the money as demanded, the boy will be released safely within three hours.

Two Desperate[8] Men

I told Bill to entertain the kid while I walked over to the post office at Poplar Grove to mail the ransom note. Bill didn't like the idea one bit. "Take my advice," he said. "Let's pull up stakes[9] and get out of here. That kid will scalp us both."

Well, when I got back to camp, Bill and Red Chief were gone. I called once or twice, and I sat down to wait. Poor Bill! Maybe he had been scalped!

After waiting a while, I heard a rustling[10] in the bushes. There was poor Bill, looking tired and sad.

"What's the trouble, Bill?" I asked.

"I was rode," Bill said. "I was his horse for about ninety miles while he attacked the settlers. But I finally managed to get him off my back. I told him to go home. There's just a limit to what a man can take!"

Eight feet behind Bill stood Red Chief, grinning from ear to ear. He had never had so much fun.

When Bill turned around and saw the kid, I thought he'd have a heart attack. He just turned pale and sat down and began to scratch in the dirt and pick up little sticks. For over an hour I thought Bill had gone out of his mind. Poor Bill! I told him we would get the affair over by midnight and be safely on our way.

Long before midnight I went to the place where the messenger was to leave the money. I had no intentions of being caught by the sheriff, so I climbed into a tree and waited.

Exactly on time, a boy came up the road on a bicycle, located the cardboard box at the foot of the fence post, slipped a piece of paper in it, and then rode away.

I waited an hour before I slipped down from the tree. I got the note and went back to the cave. Bill and I read the note by lantern light. It said:

Two Desperate Men:

Gentlemen: I received your letter today. In regard to the ransom, I must say you are a little high. I am making you a better offer, which I think you will accept. You bring Johnny home and pay me two hundred and fifty dollars, and I agree to take him off your hands. You had better come at night, for the neighbors believe he is lost for good, and I couldn't be responsible for what they may do to you if they saw you bringing him back.

Very respectfully,
Ebenezer Dorset

"Of all the nerve!" I thought to myself.

But I glanced at Bill, and hesitated. He had the saddest look in his eyes that I ever saw on the face of a sick man.

Bill said, "What's two hundred and fifty dollars, after all? We've got the money. I think Mr. Dorset's offer is more than fair."

"Tell you the truth, Bill," I said, "we've had enough trouble. We'll take him home, pay the ransom, and make our getaway."

We took Red Chief home that night. He put up a howl and didn't want to go because he had already planned an attack on another paleface fort. But we told him his father was going to get him a rifle, and we would hunt bears the next day.

It was just at midnight when we went to the Dorset home. Bill counted out two hundred and fifty dollars into Dorset's hand.

When Red Chief found out we were going to leave him, he put up an awful howl and fastened himself tight to Bill's leg. His father managed to pull him loose.

"How long can you hold him?" Bill asked.

"I am not so strong as I used to be," Dorset said, "but I think I can hold him ten minutes."

"Enough!" Bill said. "In ten minutes I'll be out of the state."

And dark as it was, and as good a runner as I am, Bill was a good mile out of town before I could catch up with him.

•Building Your Vocabulary

1.	**provisions**	food and other supplies
2.	**buggy**	a light single-seated one-horse vehicle having four wheels
3.	**christened**	gave a name, as in baptism
4.	**twined**	wound around
5.	**imp**	a little devil; a mischievous child
6.	**dote**	to be foolishly fond of

7. **dredging**   searching with a net or a drag
8. **desperate**   without hope; in great need
9. **pull up stakes**   to move to another place; to leave
10. **rustling**   a series of small sounds

• *Exercises*

A. Write an expression that will complete each sentence correctly.

1. The easiest way to get money, we thought, was to try _____.
2. Near the top of the mountain was a cave. There we stored our provisions and waited for our _____.
3. After dark I took the buggy back to the _____, where I had rented it.
4. I caught the boy and shook him until his _____ rattled.
5. It was just at _____ when we went to the Dorset home.

B. Decide whether each of the statements is true or false. Write T for *true* and F for *false*.

1. Red Chief (Johnny) was eight years old.
2. The boy was well-liked by all the townspeople.
3. The kidnappers used a car to take Johnny out of town.
4. The kidnappers offered Johnny some candy and a nice ride.
5. Johnny liked camping out and playing Indian.
6. Red Chief tried to scalp one of the kidnappers.
7. Some people dredged the river looking for Johnny.
8. Red Chief didn't want to go home.
9. The kidnappers asked for a ransom of two thousand dollars.
10. The kidnappers paid Mr. Dorset two hundred and fifty dollars to take Johnny back.

C. Write the letter of the definition in column II that most closely matches the expression in column I.

I. Word	II. Definition
1. dredging	A. a series of small sounds
2. imp	B. to move to another place; to leave
3. rustling	C. searching with a net or a drag
4. pull up stakes	D. food and other supplies
	E. gave a name, as in baptism
5. twined	F. a light single-seated one-horse ve-
6. dote	hicle having four wheels
7. christened	G. wound around
8. desperate	H. to be foolishly fond of
9. buggy	I. a little devil; a mischievous child
10. provisions	J. without hope; in great need

D. Write a paragraph or two on one of the following topics:

1. Discuss the preparations the two men made to kidnap Johnny. How did they finally manage to take him?
2. Discuss the problems that Johnny caused in the kidnapper's camp.
3. Tell how the two notes related to the kidnapping differed in their meaning.
4. Write an imaginary incident involving Johnny and Dennis the Menace.

Flight Through
the Jungle

Ralph V. Cutlip

I

Lieutenant Don Field dived his Phantom jet toward the Viet Cong[1] bunker[2] on the hilltop in a roaring burst of fury. One of his rockets hit the target, and in a second he saw a ring of sandbags, rocks, and dirt spatter into the air like a thrown egg.

As he pulled up sharply over the top of the hill, he felt a crackling sound as if lightning had struck his plane. He turned to see his left wing break open in a sheet of flame. He pressed the ejector[3] button. The thrust[4] of the explosive charge tossed him, seat and all, over a hundred feet into the air.

Don knew he had no time to lose, and he pulled the ripcord of his parachute. He wished he might have been higher and farther away, but he had no choice in the matter. A spotter plane had given him the location of the bunker, and he had attacked.

As the chute opened, he saw the ground rushing up to meet him. When he felt a sharp sting in his left leg, he knew a rifleman had him in range. He heard the report of other rifles and the sharp whistle of bullets.

Fortunately a wind current carried him away from the hill, and he began to settle to earth in a hollow that lay beyond the range of the rifle fire. Immediately below him he saw a mountain stream, and he began to pull at the lines in an effort to keep from falling into the water. The stream was wider than he had suspected, and the rapids boiled with flood water from the heavy rains of recent days.

Dropping to earth, he unfastened the chute harness quickly. Perhaps already the enemy had sent out searchers. He would have liked to hide the chute; but it lay tangled among the trees and rocks, and he realized he had no time to lose.

A path led along the stream, but he dared not follow it.

His left leg gave him no pain, but already his flight suit was soaked red on the left side, just above the knee. He felt the warmth of his lifeblood as it oozed from the wound and trickled down below the knee. He knew that great pain and soreness might come later—as soon as the nerves in his leg recovered from shock. His first problem, he thought, was to get away from the area as quickly as possible. Then he must treat the wound to stop the flow of blood and prevent infection.

He climbed the hill for two hundred yards and hid among some trees. The area reminded him of a place along a mountain trail in his native California.

Taking his sheath knife, he slashed his pants leg open. He could now see where the bullet had bit into his flesh. He felt better when he saw that the wound was not a dangerous one. Fortunately no large vein had been opened. Already the blood had begun to clot. From his first-aid kit he took a packet of sulfa compound.[5] He poured some of the powder onto the wound and then taped a bandage in place. He knew it would be all right for a while.

As he made ready to move on, he heard a man's excited voice in the deep hollow, calling to someone. Don knew little Vietnamese, but he caught the meaning of several words. One man was saying that he had found a flier's parachute, and that they would need the dogs. Now Don knew he would soon be a hunted man. He did not like the idea of being tracked by a dog like game in the jungle.

There was no time to lose. He ran, walked, and crashed through the jungle of trees and shrubbery for a mile. He found himself on a long mountain backbone that connected one hill after another in a long chain. He made no effort to conceal his trail. He had read stories about how foxes outwitted dogs with a maze[6] of trails, but his present effort was getting away as far as possible. He reckoned from the position of the late afternoon sun that he would have to turn south soon if he expected to get out of enemy country.

After an hour of walking and running, broken by brief rests, he turned toward a plain that lay southward. Once he thought he heard the barking of a dog. The sounds might have come from one of the little farms that lay along the foothills. He could not waste time guessing.

The trees, weeds, and shrubs were getting thicker. Every shrub and every tree seemed to hold out a branch or a limb that caught at his clothing, trying to hold him back. His mouth became dry with thirst, and his stomach ached from hunger. Although the heat from the afternoon sun lessened by the hour, his clothing clung to him like a wet sheet. Now . . . less than a mile behind him, he heard the long baying[7] of a dog, echoed by a second dog. The dogs were trackers—trained to hunt human beings.

Don felt the tiredness in his body as his leg muscles

began to feel as if they had been pounded. Now . . . his leg wound began to remind him that he had been hurt. The shocked nerves had come to life in a dull ache. The bandage oozed blood, but he knew the wound itself was his least worry.

The dogs came closer and closer, their noses holding to the trail easily. He felt his heart beating against his eardrums, and he began to choke. The moist, heavy air and the violent exercise had shortened his breathing to the panting of a hunted animal. For a moment he had the urge to sit, rest, and wait for the hunters.

Then he remembered some of the stories he had heard about the prison camps, and he sprang to his feet in fear. Somehow he must keep going. He knew the enemy not only had guns but they also had cords to bind his wrists behind his back, and then they would take him to a cage or a prison compound, where he would be treated little better than an animal.

Once he thought he heard the report of a heavy gun—maybe it was thunder. He wasn't sure which it was, for his mind was troubled with fear, hunger, and pain.

Having rested for a few moments, he plunged down a small hill toward the plain that lay ahead. Finally he came to another mountain stream, and he began to follow it downhill. Several hundred feet along the way he saw a fallen log that bridged the water channel from bank to bank. He walked past the log for another hundred feet. Then he thought of a fox trick he had read about once. He stepped into the water and waded back up the stream until he came to the log. He stooped and waded under it. Reaching up, he managed to climb on top of the log, where he lay for a few moments of rest. Again he heard the baying of the dogs—closer and closer. Then he saw a lightning flash over the plain below him and heard the sharp crack of thunder that shook the earth.

The promise of rain gave him new hope. It would cool

the air for the rest of the day, and it would dampen his trail. He rose to his feet and climbed the steep slope of the hill. By the time he reached the top he was out of breath. He lay down, feeling the weakness in his legs and the hunger in his stomach. From where he lay, he could see the log. Another minute passed and he dozed, to be awakened by the barking of a dog. He saw two men leading the dogs on long leashes. The men carried guns and were dressed in drab uniforms that looked little better than pajamas. Don smiled for a moment, and then his face grew serious. Never before had he been so close to the enemy.

He watched the dogs sniff at the end of the log and then go on down the hill, following his trail. He listened for several minutes as the woodland area became quiet. He could not believe his good luck. Had the enemy left him in the mountains, believing that he had continued downstream?

He waited several minutes, resting and listening to the distant thunder. The lightning flashes became more frequent, and he prayed for rain. Pulling himself together, he walked and ran toward the plain, staying as far away as he could from the watercourse.

When he reached level ground, walking was easier; but he realized he was now in the open and might be seen easily. Coming to a rice field, where the green grain stood waist high, he bent low and ran along a narrow path that led to a little shed. Already the storm had come. The shed had no doors, but he was out of the rain that began to hammer on the tin roof in a great downpour.

He was thankful for the rain. Even if the dogs had picked up his trail in the hills, he knew the rain would have drowned his scent by this time. One hundred yards away was a small house. He was sure that he heard voices and the barking of a dog, and he feared that the enemy was not far away.

In the dim light he worked fast. First he checked his wound. Although it was sore and still oozed blood in one place, he saw no signs of infection. Again he dusted it with sulfa and applied a bandage.

Several large threshing mats[8] leaned against a side wall. On another wall, out of the reach of mice, dozens of grain sacks hung.

One corner of the shed was cluttered with smaller mats and baskets of different sizes.

He grabbed an armful of the sacks and crawled behind the mats that leaned against the wall. By the time he had spread out some of the sacks onto the ground for a bed, he felt the chill of the rain. He covered his body with the rest of the sacks, and he was pleased with the return of warmth and comfort. He liked the sound of the rain. Although he still felt the pain of hunger, he rested and slept.

In the middle of the night he awoke in a daze. He was sure he heard running footsteps and the barking of dogs. He lay quietly, listening and hearing nothing but the rain. The storm was no longer a downpour. It was gentle and musical, inviting sleep.

A little while later he jerked awake. He was sure he had heard shouting voices and the barking of dogs. But the night was quiet except for the drip . . . drip . . . of the water from the tin roof to the ground below. He didn't know if he had been dreaming or not.

II

It was late morning. He awoke to a strange sound. It was laughter. He lay quiet for a moment; and when his eyes opened fully, he saw a girl looking down at him, with her face muscles dancing in amusement.

At first he was frightened by the sound of her voice and by the fact he had been surprised so easily.

He managed a smile and said, "Hi, what's so funny?"

"You . . . you . . . sleep well?" she asked in broken English.

"Yes, I guess so," he replied, "except for the barking dogs and the noise of the men who were after me."

"No dogs—no men near farm all night," she said. And then she laughed again. "You make sound like buzz saw. Maybe you scared yourself."

"Well, maybe you're right," Don said as he crawled out of his hiding place.

"You American?" she asked. Then she added quickly, "You flier?"

"Yes, how do you know?" Don asked.

"I know uniform. You must not stay here. Viet Cong may come and take you away. You hungry?"

"Yes," Don answered. "I could eat an elephant."

"You have big appetite," she said. "Come to house. I find something, but we no have elephant."

Don thought he had never seen such a pretty girl since he had left home. She was tall for one of her race. Her smooth, burnished[9] face was tinted lightly by a blush she could not hide. Her eyes, dark as night, held him in a strange mystery. Her long dark hair fell backward over her shoulders like a soft velvet scarf, hiding some of the faded blouse, which was tucked inside her work jeans. She looked as clean and as sweet as an angel.

"I'm Choi," she said. "What's your name?"

"I'm Don Field," he said. "U.S. Air Force. Right now I'm lost and hungry."

"Come. We find food," she said.

The house she led him to was not much better than the shed they had just left. The door opened outward when she pulled at a knob. There were two rooms, one separated from the other by a bamboo screen. The floor of the first room was covered with clean mats. An open closet showed where bed clothing and many other things were kept. Nobody else was in the house at the time.

A small sheet metal stove stood in one corner of the room. Two covered cooking pots sat on the warm lids.

As Choi got a bowl from the closet and filled it with rice and stewed chicken from the pots, she explained that her parents had gone to the village.

"I have two brothers. They in army. They learn to fly like you," she said proudly. "We South Vietnamese."

She handed him the bowl, and he began to eat with his fingers. He thought it was the best food he had ever tasted.

"I make some hot tea," she said. "You want?"

"No, no," Don replied. "Thank you."

At that moment the girl jumped to her feet. "Wait here!" she exclaimed. "Somebody come. Keep quiet."

She ran outside.

He finished eating quickly, not knowing what to expect.

In a few moments she ran back into the house, out of breath.

"You must go now!" she said. "Enemy soldiers come. Maybe they look for you."

She went to the closet, stood on tiptoe, reached her hand under the bedding as far as she could reach and withdrew a flashlight.

"You need this in tunnel," she said. "Come, I show you."

Puzzled beyond belief, Don took the flashlight and followed her.

"How do you know soldiers are coming?" he asked.

"Boy come down jungle path. He watch mountain road. He tell me."

Still puzzled, he followed Choi back to the shed, where she had found him that morning.

"You go now. Go fast," she said quietly as she began

to move some of the baskets and the mats in the corner of the room.

She raised a mat, and Don saw an opening in the hard-packed earth.

"You go to end of tunnel. It come out in bamboo jungle near river. Go through bamboo till you come to rice paddies.[10] Keep going till you come to road. Please leave flashlight in box at end of tunnel."

Don looked at Choi, and for the first time since childhood he felt tears in his eyes.

"Thank you, Choi," he said, as he bent and kissed her on the cheek. "I come to see you again some day."

"You come," she said. "Maybe war not last forever. Good luck . . . you say."

III

Don dropped into the hole, which was deeper than he expected. He switched on the light. The tunnel was almost three feet high. It had been dug through a heavy, dark clay. He found that he could move fairly fast on his hands and knees, but he almost gave up hope of ever reaching the end. In several different places he saw overhead exits, covered with boards or mats. There were side tunnels that sloped down to the main one. From time to time he could feel fresh air drafts. He guessed the tunnels had been dug a long time ago—perhaps during the time the French ruled the country.

Finally coming to the end of the tunnel, he found the box in which he had been told to leave the flashlight. The overhead exit was covered with a bamboo frame, wired together. Beyond the frame, he saw more bamboo tied to the framework in some way.

He pushed against the door with his left hand. It did not move. He pushed with both hands. Still it did not move.

He began to wonder if he had been trapped, like a rat in a hole.

Fear began to struggle for control of his senses. He turned his head aside and pushed with his left shoulder against the trapdoor. He felt it move upward, and he saw the daylight. Dropping to his knees, he placed the flashlight in the box. Again he pushed against the overhead door, and he heard the rustle of leaves and sticks. Coming to the outside at last, he was amazed to find himself in bamboo so thick he could scarcely move. Quickly he replaced the dead sticks and leaves to hide the tunnel opening. Then he began to twist and squirm his way through the jungle.

Progress through the tall, heavy bamboo was slow and painful. In some places the jungle was almost as dark as the tunnel he had just abandoned.

Once he thought he heard the excited voices of men, and he feared that he was being followed. He sat down and leaned against a good-sized bamboo stalk and spread out his legs quietly for a rest. Again he heard loud voices and the sounds of padding footsteps. The voices passed on, and he waited in the semidarkness as quietly as the stick that lay between two bamboo sprouts. Strangely he had not seen the stick when he had sat down, but he realized once again that his eyes had to adjust to the dim jungle light. A bird called sharply from a nearby bush, and Don turned his head and strained his eyes, trying to locate the bird. A few moments passed, and then he looked back to where his legs lay on the jungle carpet of dead sticks and leaves. Again he saw the strange-looking stick between the bamboo sprouts. This time the stick seemed longer and straighter. The stick was now crawling in a slow motion toward his right ankle, and Don realized he saw a jungle snake, a cobra—a thing far more dangerous than any Viet Cong enemy. His first impulse was to snap his feet back quickly, but his better judgment told him that it was too late for such a bold action.

He continued to lie quietly, scarcely daring to breathe. As the snake slid over his right ankle, he felt a slight tugging motion as if a rope were being pulled across his leg. In another moment the monster had started across his left leg. It was, indeed, a monster! Inch by inch, it glided from its hiding place among the bamboo sprouts. Now he could feel the dragging motion on his shins as the snake began to crawl toward his left hand, where it lay on the ground. Inch by inch it came closer to his hand. He was sure it could hear him breathing, as his chest and stomach tightened into a knot of fear. Again he had the impulse to lift his legs quickly and fling the thing into the air. Nothing in his life had ever been so frightful—not even his ejection from his burning plane. The fear that held his muscles numbly probably saved his life.

For some unknown reason the cobra turned away, and Don watched the head disappear over a piece of fallen bamboo. Don thought his body would explode as the ropelike thing of horror glided along with scarcely a sound. The entire length of the snake must have been more than eight feet. Finally when the tail disappeared, Don jumped to his feet with a cry that he had to choke with his hand.

He listened quietly for a few minutes, fearing that an enemy might have heard him. He breathed deeply and stretched his legs to relax his muscles. It had been a horrible experience, and he wanted to get out of the area as quickly as possible.

He pushed on through the jungle for several feet, and he came to an open path. He waited a few minutes before entering the path. The day was quiet except for the buzzing of insects.

The path led him to the rice paddies Choi had described.

Keeping his head down, he ran along the water ditches. In one place he crawled on all fours past some shacks, praying there would be no dog to betray him.

It took him more than an hour to go two miles. He had

begun to feel he was lost. Then he heard a truck roaring along. It was followed closely behind by another, then another. He began to run toward the road, conscious of his sore leg every step of the way.

Coming to the edge of the road, he saw a U.S. Army truck rush by. He saw another one coming less than a hundred yards away, and he ran into the middle of the road and began to wave his arms wildly.

On and on the truck came without stopping. He stepped aside quickly to avoid being crushed. Even so he felt the wind from the rushing truck. He turned to see another one tearing down upon him. Again he waved his arms wildly.

The truck ground to a stop with howling brakes.

The driver looked down and called, "Welcome aboard, sir. For a moment I thought I was running into the Viet Cong."

"Thanks for stopping," Don said. "I'd almost given up hope of ever getting back to base. Ever since I lost my plane, I've been running and hiding in a wild game of hide-and-seek."

"Sounds like some kind of nightmare," the driver said.

Don smiled. He remembered his strange adventure as being both a nightmare and a pleasant dream. He hoped to forget the nightmare of his flight through the jungle, but he knew there was no end to the dream—the dream that would continue until the day he would go back to see Choi again.

• Building Your Vocabulary

1.	**Viet Cong**	a Communist military group in South Vietnam
2.	**bunker**	a fortified place, mostly below ground
3.	**ejector**	a device to throw a pilot clear of a badly damaged plane
4.	**thrust**	a forward or upward push

5. **sulfa compound**   medicine used to kill germs
6. **maze**   a confusing network of paths
7. **baying**   barking in deep, drawn-out tones
8. **threshing mats**   large mats on which grain is beaten from the stalks
9. **burnished**   shiny; brownish in color
10. **paddies**   rice fields

• *Exercises*

A. Write an expression that will complete each sentence correctly.

1. Don knew he had no time to lose, and he pulled the _____ of his parachute.
2. From his first-aid kit he took a packet of _____.
3. His mouth became dry with thirst, and his stomach ached from _____.
4. Her smooth, burnished face was tinted lightly by a _____ she could not hide.
5. She handed him the _____, and he began to eat with his fingers.

B. Decide whether each of the following statements is true or false. Write T for *true* and F for *false*.

1. As soon as Don dropped to earth, he hid his parachute.
2. For a moment he had the urge to sit, rest, and wait for the hunters.
3. When Don came to a fallen log across a stream, he walked across the log.
4. Don hoped that it would not rain.
5. The shed in which he hid had no doors.
6. He awoke in the middle of the night. He thought he had heard footsteps and the barking of dogs.

7. Choi had two brothers in the South Vietnamese Army.
8. Choi told Don how he could escape through a tunnel.
9. Don had to crawl through the tunnel in complete darkness.
10. None of the trucks stopped to give Don a lift.

C. Write the letter of the definition in column II that most closely matches each expression in column I.

I. Word	**II. Definition**
1. maze	A. rice fields
2. thrust	B. a confusing network of paths
3. baying	C. a fortified place, mostly below
4. threshing	ground
mats	D. shiny; brownish in color
5. burnished	E. barking in deep, drawn-out tones
6. bunker	F. a device to throw a pilot clear of a
7. ejector	badly damaged plane
8. sulfa	G. a Communist military group in
compound	South Vietnam
9. Viet Cong	H. a forward or upward push
10. paddies	I. large mats on which grain is beaten
	from the stalks
	J. medicine used to kill germs

D. Write a paragraph or two on one of the following topics:
1. Tell how Lieutenant Don Field was wounded and how he tried to treat the wound.
2. Tell how Don tried to escape from the hunters in the hills.
3. Describe Choi, and tell how she tried to help Don.
4. Tell about Don's escape through the tunnel.

A Terribly Strange Bed

Wilkie Collins

It was late when my train pulled into the station. For several minutes I sat in the waiting room, not knowing what to do. I knew it was a mistake to be carrying such a large sum of money on my person at that time of night, but I had no choice in the matter. I had hoped to get to my Paris bank before it closed for the day, but my train had been caught behind a wreck and I was delayed.

Across the street from the railroad station stood a second-class hotel outlined in the dim light of a gloomy street lamp. There was no question about it—I knew that I must get off the street as soon as possible. I had heard many stories of innocent people being waylaid[1] and robbed in these darkened streets.

I decided to try the hotel.

When I crossed the street and entered the lobby, I discovered that most of the first floor was used as a gambling house. Through glass doors I saw many people at the tables

125

playing cards and throwing dice, and I heard the faint sounds of spinning roulette wheels.

My first thought was of the risk of sleeping all night in a gambling house; my second was the danger of being on the streets of Paris alone. But I had slept in worse places than this on my travels, and I knew I had to make the best of it.

Out of force of habit I felt for the money belt around my waist, and I buttoned my coat carefully. The night clerk gave me a room and I climbed the stairs, walked a long hallway, found the room, and locked myself in. Immediately I felt safer—anyway, I was glad to be off the streets. Still I had fears, and I wished the money were safe in a bank vault.

I could not put the fears out of my mind. I looked under the bed and in the closet, and I tried the fastening on the window. Then, satisfied that I had done my best for my own safety, I took off my outer clothing, put my money belt under my pillow, and went to bed.

I soon felt that I could not go to sleep. Moreover, I could not even close my eyes. I was wide awake and every nerve was alert.[2] I tossed and rolled and tried every position on the bed, yet sleep would not come. I groaned, knowing that I was in for a sleepless night.

What could I do? I had no book to read. I had no medicine that would make me sleep. I thought of all kinds of bad things. I raised myself on my elbows and looked about the room, which was lighted with beautiful moonlight that made strange shadows. The more I looked at the shadows, the more fearful I became.

The bed I was lying on was a large four-poster, covered with a canopy[3] that rested on the posts. The canopy had a valance[4] and side curtains that enclosed the bed completely, but I had drawn the curtains aside when I first got into the room. There was a dressing table, together with a tall chest of drawers, a washstand, and two straight chairs. Near the bed stood an armchair on which I had laid my clothes and necktie.

On a sidewall in full view and fully lighted by the moon was a strange-looking picture. It was a painting of a Spanish gentleman wearing a tall hat. The crown of the hat was shaped like a cone, topped with five feathers. I smiled for the first time that night, knowing that today only a woman would wear that kind of hat. The fellow had every appearance of a villain, and he looked upward as though he faced a judge or the gallows.[5]

For some reason the beautiful moonlight reminded me of a peaceful valley in England. Then I remembered a charming young lady and the good time we had had at a picnic, followed by a drive along country lanes. I most certainly must have been dreaming, for I suddenly found myself looking hard at the picture again.

Looking for what?

Good heavens! What had happened? Where were the feathers on the hat? I could no longer see the feathers. The hat was gone!

I looked again. I watched the man's face slowly disappear above the top of the bed. Now I could see only the point of his chin; finally his chest and waist. Was I dreaming? Was I mad? Was the picture being pulled up from my sight, or was the bed canopy moving down?

My heart seemed to stand still. A deadly coldness stole over me as I turned my head around on the pillow, trying to see whether or not the bed was moving. The next look in the direction of the picture was enough. The valance of the bed had now passed below his waist. And surely and slowly I saw the figure in the picture and the bottom of the frame disappear.

I am not a timid[6] person, but as I looked up toward

the canopy and realized it was slowly moving down upon me, I felt helpless. It was intended that the bed would smother me where I lay.

I looked up, speechless and breathless. Down and down —without a sound came the top of the bed, and still my fears seemed to bind me faster and faster to the mattress on which I lay. Down, down it came until I could smell the dusty odor of the canopy. In a few moments I would be dead—smothered to death by a strange bed.

In an effort to save my life, I moved at last. There was just enough room for me to roll sideways off the bed onto the floor. There I lay quietly, and with the sweat dripping from my face, I watched the canopy come down slowly.

Down it came to press tightly against the mattress. It was so close that there was not room now to squeeze my hand between it and the mattress.

I could see now that it was no ordinary bed canopy. It was a thick, broad mattress fastened to a stout frame. In the middle of the frame was a huge wooden screw like those used in wine presses. The screw reached down from a hole in the ceiling. The frightful apparatus[7] worked smoothly without a sound. As I looked on, I could not breathe, I could not move; but as I began to recover the power of thinking, I realized the awful danger I had escaped. Why was I to be the victim of murder? Had unseen eyes watched me hide my money? Surely there was no other reason to kill me.

Suddenly the canopy began to move once more. The villains who worked the machine from the room above evidently thought they had finished with me. Slowly and quietly the canopy rose to the top of the four bedposts.

Now, for the first time, I was able to move. I put on my clothes quickly, expecting any moment to have the door burst open and the thugs[8] try to make a quick end to their bad business.

It was my intention to get out of the room alive. Looking

out the window, I saw a drainpipe. I knew that I could slide down the pipe and escape. I raised the window slowly without making a sound. I had already got one leg over the windowsill when I remembered the money belt. I went back for it. I was now determined to escape alive and save my money too.

Once outside the window, it was a small trick to slide down the drainpipe, and I hurried away to a police station.

I told my story to the captain of police. He immediately ordered an investigation. Every person within the building was held and questioned. The villains were caught before the night was over.

After I identified the room and the strange bed, the captain led the way into the room above. He stamped on the floor and then ordered the floor boards to be taken up. Lights were brought, and we saw a deep cavity[9] between the floor of this room and the ceiling of the room below. Here was the place the robbers had worked the screw that lowered and raised the bed canopy. A secret passageway led to a hallway closet.

Later, as I gave a full report of my experience to the police captain, I asked, "Do you think that anybody has been murdered in that bed in the same way that they tried to kill me?"

"Without a doubt," he said. "I have often seen drowned men laid out at the morgue[10] in whose pockets suicide notes were found, saying that they had lost everything at a gaming table and could not go home to face the truth. Evidently many of the poor victims had won heavily and had been persuaded to spend the rest of the night in the room and were smothered to death in their sleep. Later their bodies were thrown into the river after the murderers had written suicide notes and had placed them in the pockets of the victims."

"How did the villains suspect me?" I asked.

"The clerk had some reason to think you had money. He passed the word along. You are a lucky man, sir. And you have helped to expose an awful thing."

● *Building Your Vocabulary*

1. **waylaid**   attacked by surprise
2. **alert**   quick to respond; watchful
3. **canopy**   a covering over a bed
4. **valance**   a short drapery hanging from the canopy of a bed or from a window
5. **gallows**   an upright frame used in hanging criminals
6. **timid**   afraid; lacking courage
7. **apparatus**   equipment; a machine
8. **thugs**   brutal men; criminals
9. **cavity**   a hollow place
10. **morgue**   a place where the bodies of persons found dead are kept for identification

● *Exercises*

A. Write the letter of the expression that best completes each of the following statements:

1. When the man entered the hotel, he saw many people _____.

   a. at dinner in a dining room
   b. talking together in the lobby
   c. playing cards and throwing dice

2. Out of force of habit the man _____.

   a. felt for the money belt
   b. wound his watch
   c. took off his topcoat

3. As soon as the man had locked the door of his room, he _____.

   a. looked under the bed
   b. washed his face and hands
   c. set an armchair against the door

4. The man could not go to sleep because he _____.
   a. felt the bed moving
   b. heard noises downstairs
   c. thought of all kinds of bad things
5. The strange-looking picture on the wall was fully lighted by _____.
   a. a gas lamp
   b. the moonlight
   c. a streetlight

B. Decide whether each of the following statements is true or false. Write T for *true* and F for *false*.
1. The train was late because of a wreck.
2. The man had to walk several blocks to find a hotel.
3. The man got a room in a first-class hotel.
4. The room was completely dark except for a gaslight.
5. Before going to bed, the man hid his money belt under a pillow.
6. For a while the man could not move as he watched the bed canopy come down.
7. The man saved his life by rolling onto the floor.
8. While the man lay quietly on the floor, he watched the canopy rise to the top of the bedposts.
9. The man escaped by climbing down a ladder.
10. The police captain said he believed that many men had been murdered in the room.

C. Write a paragraph or two on one of the following topics:
1. Tell why the man had to stay in the hotel for the night. Why did he have fears?
2. Describe the strange room.
3. In your own words describe the man's experiences in the strange bed.
4. Tell how the man escaped and what happened after he went to the police station.

D. Write the letter of the definition in column II that most closely matches each word in column I.

I. Word	II. Definition
1. morgue	A. a hollow place
2. waylaid	B. brutal men; criminals
3. valance	C. an upright frame used in hanging criminals
4. timid	
5. alert	D. attacked by surprise
6. gallows	E. afraid; lacking courage
7. apparatus	F. a covering over a bed
8. thugs	G. quick to respond; watchful
9. canopy	H. a place where the bodies of persons found dead are kept for identification
10. cavity	
	I. equipment; a machine
	J. a short drapery hanging from the canopy of a bed or from a window

Written in the Stars

Lois Duncan

Ever since I was very little I knew some day my prince would come. I used to imagine his riding up on a snow-white horse to scoop me up and carry me away to his castle. Of course, as I grew older I gave up this fairy-tale idea, but I knew that somewhere in the world there was a Special Person looking for me just as I was looking for him. It had to happen; it was written in the stars.

I never talked much about my dreams except to Mother. Oh, I had a few dates with silly boys once in awhile, just to kill time until that Special Person arrived.

He arrived when I was seventeen. He was Ted Bennington, a new boy in our neighborhood.

Several things led up to my getting to know Ted.

For my birthday Mother gave me a locket.[1] When I opened the package I was surprised. The locket was not new. It was something she had prized[2] many years. I had often seen it. In fact, every time I opened Mother's jewelry box looking for a pair of earrings or a bracelet to borrow, I saw it in its special place, together with some of the things that Daddy had given her.

There was the whole story of a romance in that box—Daddy's track medals, his fraternity[3] pin, some gift pins, and the silver bars[4] he wore when he was in the Navy.

"But, Mother," I said, "do you really mean for me to have this? It belongs to you."

"Indeed I do," Mother said. "It does mean a lot to me, but I've always said my daughter should have it when she became seventeen." There was a faraway look in her eyes I did not understand.

"But why seventeen?" I asked. "That's hardly a milestone[5] in one's life."

"It was to me," Mother said. "It was the age of heartbreak."

I looked at her in disbelief. "Your heart was never broken," I said.

It was impossible to think of Daddy, with his warm gray eyes and gentle smile, ever breaking anyone's heart, least of all Mother's. Daddy and Mother had had a beautiful marriage. They always seemed to have fun together. But Daddy had died two years ago.

"Oh, it was broken, all right," Mother said lightly. "And yours may be too, dear. It often happens that way."

I laughed to myself. I didn't quite understand what Mother was talking about. But I did love the locket. It was tiny and heart-shaped, held by a thin gold chain, and it was lovely.

The locket wasn't the only gift I received. Besides that Mother gave me an evening dress. And Nancy, my best friend, gave me a pair of rose slippers to wear with it. But the gift that caused my heart to beat faster was a simple blue scarf with a gold border. It came from Ted Bennington.

"I hope you like it," he said. "I don't know much about picking out presents for girls."

"I love it," I said. "It's just beautiful!"

I liked the gift, but I liked Ted himself even more. I liked the way his blond, curly hair fell over his forehead, and his honest blue eyes and nice square chin. I liked his being shy and sweet and serious. He was so different from the smooth know-it-alls in our senior class.

I had begun noticing Ted about two months before. He had been in my class one month, and I hadn't paid him any attention. In fact, nobody paid him any attention. He was a quiet boy, and he wasn't on any of the school teams. He worked after school and on weekends in a drugstore. I think that might have made him shy, having to work when other kids goofed around.

I didn't have a date for the Homecoming Dance,[6] and I was on the lookout for someone to take me. You don't have too much choice when you're a senior and most of the senior boys are going steady with juniors and sophomores. So I made a list of the boys who were left and crossed off the ones who were too short, and that left only four. Ronny Brice weighs three hundred pounds, and Steven Salerno can't stand me, and Stanley Pierce spits when he talks. Only Ted was left.

Ted Bennington, I thought, you may not know it yet, but you are going to take me to the Homecoming Dance.

And I managed it. I spoke to him and smiled every time I had a chance. As we left class each day, I just happened to be at the door when he came out. A week or two of that and then the big step. "Nancy's having a party this weekend, Ted, a girl-ask-boy affair. Would you like to go?" It was really pretty easy.

Ted was standing at his locker when I asked him. He turned and looked surprised as though he had not heard me correctly.

"Go? You mean with you?" he asked.

"Yes, Ted, I'm talking to you," I said.

"Why—why, sure. Thanks. I'd like to," he said.

He looked so pleased I wondered if he had ever taken a girl anywhere in his entire life. Then I began to think I'd made a mistake. Would the Crowd like him? The Crowd were the school leaders, the group I'd known since childhood. And Ted wasn't one of them.

But it was too late then, of course, to back out, so I let it go, trying not to worry too much as the week ended. On Saturday night at eight sharp Ted arrived at my house.

He made a good impression on Mother. He was neat and polite, and I knew by the way Mother acted that she liked him.

Ted didn't have a car, so we walked to Nancy's house, and it was a nice walk. Everything went very well at the party. Ted really made an effort to fit in. He danced and took part in the games and talked to people.

Even Nancy was surprised.

"You know," she said when we were out in the kitchen together getting some Cokes, "that Ted Bennington—he's really a nice boy. How come we've overlooked him so long?"

I said, "I don't know. I was wondering the same thing myself."

I wondered even more as we walked home after the party. He asked me what I was going to do after graduation. I told him I was going to secretarial school, and he said he was working for a scholarship to Tulane, where he planned to study medicine. I learned that he had three sisters, that his mother was a widow like mine, and that he enjoyed playing the guitar. The moonlight was beautiful, and suddenly I was quite conscious[7] of my hand, small and empty, swinging along beside me. His hand was swinging, too, and after awhile they sort of bumped into each other. We walked the rest of the way without saying much, just holding hands and walking along in the moonlight.

Ted took me to the Homecoming Dance. It just seemed

the natural thing to do. And by this time I knew that Ted was that very Special Person I had dreamed about. It grew out of our walks together, long hikes through the autumn woods with the trees blowing wild and red and gold against the blue sky, and picnics with the Crowd. Sometimes Ted brought his guitar to the picnics, and we all sang.

"Why didn't you tell us you played the guitar?" somebody asked him.

Ted grinned and said, "I didn't think anybody would be interested."

By then we were spending almost all our time together. I had never felt this way about any boy before.

Ted said, "You and I get along together so well. It seems as if it were meant to be that way."

"You mean," I said—and I didn't know how to say it —'you mean it's as though it is written in the stars?"

Ted was silent a moment and then he said, "Yes, that's what I mean."

It was the night of the Senior Prom. I wore my new rose evening dress, my rose slippers, and the locket Mother had given me.

Ted noticed it right away. "Nice," he commented. "Is it a family treasure?"

"More or less," I said. "Daddy gave it to Mother, and Mother gave it to me."

"Does it open?" he asked.

"I don't know," I said.

"Let's see." He reached over and took the locket in his hands. In a moment he had pried[8] it open. A tiny lock of hair fell out.

"So," he said, smiling. "I didn't know your father had red hair."

"I guess he must have when he was young. Put it back, Ted. It belongs there."

He did so, closing the locket gently.

I'd tell you about the summer, but you must know already what it's like to be in love. You get up in the morning and eat breakfast just as you always have done before, but every moment you are thinking, "I am going to see him today—in two hours—in one hour—in ten minutes—and now he is here!"

Then one day Ted had the happy news that he had received a scholarship at Tulane. "How do you like the sound of Doctor Bennington?" he asked me.

"Wonderful!" I said. "But I'll miss you."

"I'll miss you too," he said. "I wish you were going to Tulane with me."

"Don't worry," I said. "I'll be right here waiting. Maybe I can get a job at the college before you finish."

"That would be great, but I'm afraid," he said.

"Afraid of what?" I asked.

"Well, everything is so perfect, I'm afraid I'll lose you."

"You don't need to worry," I told him. "You don't lose love that is written in the stars."

But I was wrong.

Ted went away to school, and we wrote letters to each other quite often at first. Then, as the days passed, we wrote less and less. And that was the beginning of the end. He couldn't come home for Thanksgiving; and when he was home for Christmas, I had the measles.

We did not get to see each other until spring vacation. By then we had been apart so long that we spent the whole week getting to know each other again. Ted was as good and sweet and wonderful as ever, but somehow he seemed different. When he went back to school, he said, "Don't forget me."

"Of course not," I said, but this time I was not so sure.

As it worked out, it was Ted who met somebody else. She was a student at Tulane. Ted wrote me a letter telling about her. He said he was sorry, and he knew I would understand.

It was raining the day the letter came. I read it in the living room and then gave it to Mother to read and went upstairs to my room.

I lay on the bed and listened to the sound of the rain. I didn't hate Ted, but I couldn't believe what had happened. I didn't even hate the girl. I could not believe that he was now gone and he would never come back again. Never!

I was still lying there when Mother came in. Before she spoke, I knew what she was going to say.

"There are other boys," she said. "You may not believe it now, but there will be."

"I suppose so," I said, "but Ted was The One. I can never fall in love again!"

Mother was silent a moment. Then she said, "Do you have the locket I gave you?"

"The locket? Yes, of course, it's in the top drawer of the dresser."

Mother got the locket. "Put it on," she said.

I sat up and put the locket around my neck.

"You see," she said, "the locket was given to me by a Special Person—*The One*—when we were engaged."

Then I held the locket lovingly, remembering Daddy. What a happy life he and Mother had had.

"You see," she said, "he was kind, sweet, and wonderful. I was sure he was written for me in the stars." Then she added slowly, "He was killed in a train wreck three weeks after we became engaged."

"He what!" I exclaimed. "But I thought—you mean you loved somebody before Daddy—somebody you thought was The Special One?"

"Yes, that is it. If I'd married him, I'm sure that I would have been very happy. As it worked out, three years later I married your father. We loved each other, and I was happy with *him*."

"I don't understand," I said.

Then Mother replied, "What I'm trying to tell you, honey, is that there is no one special person who alone can make us happy. There are many fine people in the world. Ted is one of them, but he came along too soon."

I almost cried because I thought I was losing the dream of my childhood.

Then Mother said gently, "One of these days a good man will come along at the right time—he will be the *One* written for you in the stars."

She went out and closed the door softly and left me alone, listening to the rain.

I looked at the door Mother had just closed behind her, and I thought about the other door, the door of Hope that she had just opened.

• Building Your Vocabulary

1.	locket	a little case for holding a picture or a lock of hair, usually worn as a necklace
2.	prized	valued highly
3.	fraternity	a club for men
4.	silver bars	shoulder badges; insignia, or marks of rank
5.	milestone	an important point in progress or development
6.	Homecoming Dance	a school dance to which the alumni are invited
7.	conscious	aware
8.	pried	pulled open

• Exercises

A. Write the letter of the expression that best completes each of the following statements:

1. For the girl's birthday, her mother gave her an evening dress and a LOCKeł

   a. locket   *b*. necklace   *c*. watch

2. Ted Bennington was a _Quiet boy_
   - *a*. football hero
   - *b*. quiet boy
   - *c*. debate champion
3. Ted played the _Quitar_
   - *a*. accordion   *b*. banjo   *c*. guitar
4. The girl didn't have a date for the _~~Homecoming Dance~~_
   - *a*. Homecoming Dance
   - *b*. Senior Prom
   - *c*. Easter Ball
5. Ted hoped to get a scholarship at _Tulane_
   - *a*. Notre Dame   *b*. Harvard   *c*. Tulane

B. Decide whether each of the following statements is true or false. Write T for *true* and F for *false*.

1. Ted Bennington had lived in the same neighborhood as the girl for several years.
2. At the time of this story the girl was nineteen years old.
3. The locket was heart-shaped. **T**
4. Ted gave the girl a scarf for her birthday.
5. On weekends Ted worked in a drugstore. **T**
6. Ted was surprised when the girl asked him to take her to Nancy's party. **T**
7. Ted took the girl to the party in his car. **F**
8. Ted didn't know how to dance.
9. The girl said she planned to go to a secretarial school. **T**
10. Ted planned to study engineering in college. **F**

C. Write one or two paragraphs on one of the following topics:
   1. Describe the kind of person Ted Bennington was. Tell how he looked and how he acted.
   2. Tell how the girl got Ted to take her to Nancy's party.
   3. Tell why the locket was so important to the girl's mother. Why do you think she gave it to her daughter?

4. Think about the story and try to explain the full meaning of the title.

D. Write the letter of the definition in column II that most closely matches each expression in column I.

I. Word	**II. Definition**

1. pried
2. locket
3. prized
4. fraternity
5. Homecoming Dance
6. conscious
7. milestone
8. silver bars

A. a club for men
B. shoulder badges; insignia, or marks of rank
C. a school dance to which the alumni are invited
D. aware
E. valued highly
F. an important point in progress or development
G. pulled open
H. a little case for holding a picture or a lock of hair, usually worn as a necklace

A Fight With a Cannon

Victor Hugo

I

There were loud cries of alarm. At the same time sounds like thunder rocked the warship.

The captain and his lieutenant rushed to the companionway,[1] but they could not get down to the gun deck because all the gunners were rushing up the steps to the top deck.

Something terrible had just happened.

One of the cannons, a twenty-four pounder,[2] had just broken loose from its moorings[3] at a gun port.[4]

This is the most dangerous accident that can possibly take place on shipboard. Nothing more terrible can happen to a ship under full sail on the open sea.

A cannon that is mounted on wheels so that it can be moved back and forth for loading and firing can suddenly become a thing of evil if it breaks loose. It moves like a ball, rolling with the pitching[5] of the ship. It plunges, goes, comes, turns, and then shoots like an arrow from one end

145

of the deck to the other. It crashes, bangs, rears, dodges, and then kills.

It becomes a monster of madness. It is as quick as a panther, alert as a mouse, heavy and clumsy like an elephant. It weighs ten thousand pounds. It can spin, dart, and rebound[6] as quickly as a ball.

And what is to be done? How is one to put an end to it? How can it be captured and tied back in its place, this giant brute of metal? One can reason with a bulldog, frighten a tiger, tame a lion, but what can one do against this monster, a loose cannon? The deck beneath it gives it full swing. It is moved by the ship, which is moved by the sea, which is moved by the wind. This thing is a terrible toy. The ship, the waves, all play with it. Any one of its blows might smash a hole in the ship and sink it.

How is one to stop its terrible play? The cannon advances, backs away, strikes right and left, smashes anything in its way, and crushes men like flies.

In an instant the whole crew was on foot. Every man was running for his life. It was the fault of the gun captain, who had failed to fasten the mooring chain properly and block the four wheels of the gun carriage.[7] A heavy sea had struck, and the cannon had broken loose and had begun to run about the deck in its madness.

At the moment when the cannon broke loose, the gunners were on the gun deck. Some worked together in groups according to their duties. The cannon ran forward with the pitching of the vessel, made a gap in one group of men, killing four at the first blow. Then sliding back, it shot out again as the ship rolled and cut a fifth man in two. As the cannon ran loose, looking for more victims, the gunners fled the deck.

Then the giant gun was left alone. It had the freedom of the deck. It was its own master and master of the ship. It could do what it pleased. The whole crew, who could laugh in the fury of battle, now trembled in fear.

The captain and the lieutenant stopped at the head of the companionway, dumb, pale, and not knowing what to do.

II

Someone ran past the captain and started down the companionway. It was the admiral, an older man, wise in the ways of the sea. Half way down the steps, he stopped and looked.

The cannon was still rushing about like a hunted thing. The four wheels passed back and forth over the dead men, cutting them, slashing them, till the five bodies looked like logs of wood rolling about the deck. The cannon had already broken several holes along the gun rail and the water poured in, almost swamping the ship. The masts had been broken and damaged. Ten guns out of thirty were damaged by the mad rushes of the monster. They would be useless in case of an enemy attack.

The captain quickly recovered his presence of mind. He ordered everything that could check the cannon's mad charges to be thrown through the hatchway[8] down onto the gun deck—mattresses, bedding, spare sails, cable, and sea bags.

But what could these rags do? Nobody dared to go below to lay them in place properly. In a few minutes most of the things were reduced to lint.

The old admiral stood like a statue for a few moments. He did not move. He knew that the ship would soon be wrecked and that many lives would be lost. He heard voices on the deck above him.

"Do you believe in God, lieutenant?" the captain asked.

"Yes, sometimes."

"During a storm at sea, lieutenant?"

"Yes—most certainly in moments like this."

"God alone can save us," the captain replied.

Everybody was silent as the cannon continued to charge about the deck. Outside the waves beat against the ship. Their blows echoed the shocks of the cannon.

Suddenly, in the middle of the deck, a man appeared with an iron bar in his hand. He was the gun captain, the man whose carelessness had caused all the trouble. Having caused the mischief, he was now trying to repair it. He had grabbed the iron bar in one hand, a rope with a slip noose in the other, and had jumped down the hatchway to the gun deck.

Then began an awful scene—a contest between the gun and the gunner, a great battle of mind over matter.

The gunner braced himself in a corner and waited for the gun to pass him as the ship pitched between waves.

He knew his gun. He had lived with it. How many times had he put his hand into its mouth! It was his monster. He began to speak to it as if it were a dog.

"Come!" he said. "Come here!" Everybody watched. Nobody believed what he saw. If the monster charged, the man would surely die.

The old admiral stood quietly. Suddenly his eyes lighted up.

Beneath them the sea blindly directed the contest.

For a moment the sea was quiet and the cannon stood still.

"Come, now!" the gunner said.

The cannon seemed to listen.

Suddenly it leaped toward him. The man dodged the blow. The battle had begun.

It was now almost dark. The man needed light. The darkness mattered not to the monster that reared and charged with each motion of the vessel.

One end of the chain was left hanging to the gun carriage. The loose chain whirled in the air like a whip when the gun

charged. A single blow from the flying chain could crush a man's skull. However, the man dared the monster to attack.

"Come now! Try it again!" the gunner shouted, holding the iron bar at ready.

Again the gun roared down the deck as if intent on killing its master. Jumping quickly, the gunner took safety at the foot of the steps not far from the old man who was looking on. The cannon seemed to notice it, and without taking the trouble to turn around, slid back toward the man.

Then the admiral stepped down to the deck. With quick movements he grabbed a sea bag and threw it between the wheels of the cannon.

The sea bag acted as a clog. The cannon stumbled for a moment. The gunner, taking advantage of this opportunity, stuck his iron bar between the spokes of one of the hind wheels. As the wheel turned, the bar caught fast between the floor and the gun carriage. The cannon stopped, leaned forward, and then turned over on its side. Rushing in with all his might, the gunner passed the slip noose around the neck of the monster and tied the loose end to the rail.

The battle was ended. The mariners and sailors clapped their hands and cheered. Then the whole crew rushed forward with chains and cables, and in an instant the cannon was tied down.

The gunner saluted the old man and said, "Sir, you have saved my life."

The admiral made no reply. He climbed the companionway and returned to his cabin.

III

The man had won the battle against the gun, but the monster had all but wrecked the ship. Five men lay dead—their bodies ground to formless masses of flesh and bone. The side planking of the ship had been smashed in several places. The ship was leaking and a storm was coming.

While the crew was repairing the damage to the gun deck, the admiral had come on deck again.

He had not noticed a proceeding that had taken place on the foredeck. The lieutenant had drawn up the marines in line near the mainmast, and at a command the sailors formed in a line behind the marines.

The captain approached the admiral. Behind the captain the gunner walked, tired but looking pleased with his victory over the cannon.

The captain saluted the admiral and said, "Sir, considering what this man has done, do you not think there is something due him from his commander?"

"I think so," the admiral said.

"Please give your orders," the captain replied.

"It is for you to give them; you are the captain," the admiral said.

"But you are the admiral," the captain said.

The admiral looked at the gunner. "Come forward," he commanded.

The admiral turned toward the captain, took off the cross of Saint Louis from the captain's jacket and pinned it to the gunner's jacket.

"Hurrah! Hurrah!" the sailors shouted.

The mariners stood stiffly at attention.

And the admiral, pointing to the surprised gunner, said, "Now have this man shot."

The sailors quieted in alarm.

Then the admiral raised his voice and said: "This man's carelessness has almost destroyed this ship. In a matter of minutes the sea may swallow us. At this minute enemy ships hunt us in the darkness. We shall all surely pay for this man's carelessness with our lives. He should be rewarded for his bravery, but now he must pay the cost of his neglect. Let it be done!"

The captain nodded his head and gave an order.

A sergeant of marines gave another order. Twelve marines stepped out of line and stood in two files, six by six. The gunner, without saying a word, placed himself between the two files.

A drum began to roll in slow time. The ship's chaplain,[9] with a cross in hand, came on deck and took his place by the gunner's side.

"March!" the sergeant said. The marines, in slow step, marched to the bow of the ship.

The chaplain said the last rites[10] and stepped aside.

The sergeant gave another order. Instantly twelve guns fired in a flash of light and in a single sound.

Then there was the sound of a body falling into the sea.

• Building Your Vocabulary

1.	**companion-way**	a stairway from one deck of a ship to another deck
2.	**twenty-four pounder**	a cannon that fires a twenty-four pound ball
3.	**moorings**	a place where something is fastened
4.	**port**	an opening in the side of a ship through which a cannon can be fired
5.	**pitching**	the rising and falling of a ship in rough seas
6.	**rebound**	to come back to the same place after striking something
7.	**carriage**	a platform with wheels

8. **hatchway**　　　an opening in the deck of a ship
9. **chaplain**　　　a priest or minister assigned to the
　　　　　　　　　armed forces
10. **rites**　　　religious ceremonies

● *Exercises*

A. Write an expression that would complete each sentence correctly.

1. One of the cannons, a twenty-four pounder, had just broken loose from its _____.
2. The fact that the cannon was loose was the fault of the _____.
3. As the cannon ran loose looking for more victims, the gunners fled the _____.
4. The old admiral was wise in the ways of the _____.
5. "Do you believe in _____?" the captain asked the lieutenant.

B. Decide whether each of the following statements is true or false. Write T for *true* and F for *false*.

1. The cannon was mounted on wheels so that it could be moved back and forth for firing.
2. The cannon weighed ten thousand pounds.
3. After five men had been killed, the gunners fled the deck.
4. The ship was entirely safe once the cannon was tied down.
5. The cannon had broken loose during an enemy attack.
6. The gunner spoke to the cannon as if it were a dog.
7. The gunner knew he would not be hurt by the cannon.
8. The gunner stuck an iron bar between the spokes of one of the wheels.

9. The admiral pinned his own medal on the gunner's jacket.

10. The admiral said that the gunner had to pay for his mistake.

C. Write the letter of the definition in column II that most closely matches each expression in column I.

I. Word	II. Definition
1. rites	A. the rising and falling of a ship in rough seas
2. companion- way	B. a platform with wheels
3. chaplain	C. religious ceremonies
4. carriage	D. to come back to the same place after striking something
5. port	
6. twenty-four pounder	E. a stairway from one deck of a ship to another deck
7. pitching	F. an opening in the side of a ship through which a cannon can be fired
8. hatchway	
9. moorings	G. a priest or minister assigned to the armed forces
10. rebound	H. a cannon that fires a twenty-four-pound ball
	I. an opening in the deck of a ship
	J. a place where something is fastened

D. Write a paragraph or two on one of the following topics:

1. Tell what happened after the cannon broke loose from its moorings.

2. Tell how the gunner was able to bring the cannon under control. Who helped him? How did he help?

3. Describe the ceremony that took place on deck after the gun had been tied down.

4. Try to prove that this kind of accident could not happen on a modern warship.

The Pit
and the Pendulum

Edgar Allan Poe

I

I awoke from a deep sleep, lying on the cold, hard floor of a dungeon.[1] It was as dark as midnight. For a few minutes I tried to recall the events that led to my being put into prison. My mind was almost a blank and I was weak from hunger.

Suddenly it came to me quite clearly—first, the soldiers and then the black-robed judges of the Inquisition.[2] The judges had agreed that I must be punished and then die because I was a heretic.[3]

As long as I live, I shall never forget the seven burning candles, the seven black robes, and the seven white faces. How could I make the judges believe that I was a Christian?

The charges against me were all false! At one time I

had dared to find fault with the Inquisition and its methods of punishment. Somebody had reported my name, and now I was to pay for my folly.[4] My careless words and my politics, not my religious beliefs, had fired the jealousy[5] of the judges.

I was in the cell alone. The dungeon keepers had taken my clothes and my weapons. All I had was a robe of coarse cloth that gave me little warmth.

In an effort to find out what kind of place I was in, I rose from the floor and began to feel my way along the walls. The floor was moist and slippery. By some strange reasoning I guessed that the cell was round in shape, and that it was built of pieces of stone or metal. I could not judge correctly, for I was upset and sick unto death. I tore a piece of cloth from my robe and pushed one end into a crack in the wall. Then I continued to feel my way along, counting each step. After I had walked around the room, and my fingers once again touched the piece of cloth, I estimated that I had taken over a hundred steps inside the wall. My efforts gave me no hope, for there wasn't a single opening—not even a ray of light through the slightest crack.

My next effort was to explore the center of the cell. This I did by placing one foot before the other in slow steps. Suddenly my feet shot out from under me. The slick floor brought me down in a heavy fall. My body slid forward several feet before I came to rest.

When I began to move my arms in an effort to rise, I was surprised that I felt nothing but space. I reached out hopelessly, like a drowning man grabbing at sticks and straws.

Suddenly there was a faint light in the dungeon, and to my horror I saw that I lay at the edge of a deep pit or well, from which came a terrible odor. I lay quietly for several minutes, fearing that I would slip into the pit.

Finally overcoming some of my fear, I felt alongside my body and found a small stone, which I dropped into the pit.

It seemed several seconds before I heard the splash of water. I shuddered as I sensed how close I had come to a horrible death.

In some strange way the light had increased, and I could now see more clearly the nature of the dungeon. Its general shape was square, not circular, and it was built of large iron plates.

I rolled away from the pit and crawled back to the side wall, where I had slept after being captured and beaten. Nearby was a small pitcher of water. I drank some of it though it had the taste of watered wine. Then I slept again.

II

The water must have been drugged, for I awoke with a headache and I felt as though I had been asleep for ages. I lay on my back and I could not move my body. The reason was that I was bound to a framework by a long leather strap that held my body, legs, and right arm tightly. Only my left arm and head were free.

A dish of food was within reach of my free hand. Being quite hungry, I ate some of it eagerly. The food increased my thirst, but the water pitcher was beyond my reach. What worse punishment could one have—a dying thirst?

Looking up to the ceiling of my prison, I saw that it was built of iron plates, like the side walls. One panel had a painted figure of Father Time. Instead of a scythe, [6] Father Time held a huge pendulum, such as we see on old clocks. While I gazed at it, one end of the pendulum dropped down from the ceiling and began to swing back and forth. I watched it several minutes, more in wonder than in fear. I had not yet guessed its importance.

A slight noise attracted my attention, and looking at the floor, I saw several rats running about. They had come from the well and their secret holes, lured[7] by the smell of the food. Even as I watched, more rats joined the pack, and I had to make an effort with my free hand to scare them away.

I must have lain there half an hour when I again looked upward. A hissing sound warned me of danger. I was amazed to see that the pendulum had come closer in its broad sweep. Again I felt the awful fear of death when I realized that the pendulum itself was a crescent-shaped[8] knife.

There was no longer any question about the doom the Inquisition had prepared for me. No fate could be worse than falling into the horrible pit, but now I faced a new danger.

Down—the blade came, swinging back and forth, far and wide. As I watched it in terror, I saw that with each motion it came closer to my breast.

Down—the blade swung and hissed, aimed at my heart. It was hope that held my nerves from shock. It was

hope that kept me alive, facing this devilish machine of slow death.

Down—the blade swung, now barely two feet from my body. I was sure that I could smell the cold steel as it reached to make the final strokes.

Down—down it came! I struggled to free my shoulders. My left arm was free to my left shoulder. I could reach my food dish but no farther. Had I been able to break the strap that held my right arm, I might have grabbed hold of the pendulum and stopped it.

However, the machine was lowering the pendulum slowly, and I saw that it would take some time for the blade to cut through my robe—then it would be my flesh, my ribs, and then my heart.

Down—down it came and now I could see the hissing blade barely a foot above me.

For many hours the framework upon which I lay had been swarming with rats. They had been able to steal most of my food in the dish. In my efforts to scare them away, my hand waved in a seesaw motion. In their great hunger they had bitten my fingers and the end of my nose. Then a thought came to me—a prayerful hope.

With the pieces of food that remained in the dish, I rubbed the strap wherever I could reach it. Then I lay still. At first the rats didn't understand why I kept quiet. Then a bold one leaped upon the framework and smelled the strap. That was a signal for a general rush. Forth from the well they hurried in fresh troops and began to gnaw at the strap in many places. They ran over me boldly. Their foul odor filled me with horror and disgust. I became so sick that I would have welcomed a quick stroke of the death-dealing blade.

The movement of the blade did not bother them. Avoiding its strokes, they gnawed the strap into pieces.

At last I was free—not a moment too soon. The next stroke of the blade cut through my robe and I felt a sharp sting of pain. There was not a moment to lose! Before the pendulum swung on its backward stroke, I rolled off the framework onto the floor. For a moment, at least, I was free.

III

Did I say I was free? The very moment I rolled away from the trap, some unseen force stopped the pendulum, and I watched it being drawn through an opening in the ceiling. Free? Twice I had escaped death, but now I became aware that I faced death in another way, for already the light within the cell changed into a strange glow. The iron plates were being heated in some way I knew not how. I felt the warmth that came from them. I sat on the floor as if in a dream. The cell was getting hotter and I could smell the hot iron.

A second change was taking place in my prison. The hot walls were moving toward me, forcing me to the center of the cell. As the walls began to glow, my lungs struggled with the hot air. Would it not be better to hurl myself into the pit and drown in its cool waters than to suffer the burning pain of hot iron?

Then I smelled the foul[9] odor of the pit and thought of the countless hundreds of rats. "Death," I cried, "any death but that of the pit!" Fool! I knew the object of the burning iron was to force me into the pit.

I pulled back—but the closing walls pressed me closer to the hole. At length there wasn't an extra inch of solid ground left for me. I could not fight much longer, for I had lost the will to live. I cried out in my despair.[10]

I dropped to my knees, knowing that in a few seconds my body would be falling into the dark waters below.

Was it a dream? No, it was real—I heard a hum of human voices. Then there was a loud blast of trumpets! Then I heard a sound like thunder! The fiery walls were moving back!

Suddenly the dungeon was fully lighted, and a friendly arm pulled me from the edge of the pit. The helping hand was that of General La Salle of the French army. The army had entered Toledo [Spain] and had captured the headquarters of the Inquisition. I was lucky that the French had come in time!

• Building Your Vocabulary

1.	dungeon	a dark underground prison
2.	Inquisition	a church group that punished disbe-lievers
3.	heretic	one who does not believe in the teach-ings of the church
4.	folly	foolishness
5.	jealousy	ill feeling arising from distrust or envy of another
6.	scythe	a curved blade fastened to a curved handle; used in mowing hay
7.	lured	tempted
8.	crescent-shaped	shaped like the moon in its first quarter
9.	foul	bad; nasty
10.	despair	loss of hope

• Exercises

A. Write the letter of the expression that best completes each of the following statements:

1. The man was accused of being a _____.
   a. robber   b. murderer   c. heretic
2. The dungeon in which the man was imprisoned was made of _____.

a. wooden beams   *b*. concrete   *c*. iron plates
3. Father Time seemed to be swinging a _____.
    a. scythe   *b*. pendulum   *c*. sword
4. The prisoner was fastened to a framework by a
_____.
    a. leather strap   *b*. rope   *c*. piece of wire
5. The prisoner was rescued by the army of _____.
    a. Spain   *b*. England   *c*. France

B. Decide whether each of the following statements is true or false. Write T for *true* and F for *false*.
1. The judges who said the man must be punished wore white robes.
2. The man did not believe in the religion of his church.
3. The man took over three hundred steps around the inside of the prison.
4. When the man fell, he slid to the edge of the pit.
5. After the man fell, there was suddenly a faint light in the dungeon.
6. The man thought the water he drank had been drugged.
7. The man was bound to the framework tightly. Only his right arm was left free.
8. The man was afraid to eat the food that was left for him.
9. The movement of the pendulum did not scare the rats.
10. The man thought no fate could be worse than falling into the horrible pit.

C. Write a paragraph or two on one of the following topics:
1. In your own words describe the dungeon. Why was it such a terrible place?
2. Tell how the man nearly fell into the pit.
3. Tell how the man managed to escape the pendulum.

4. Try to imagine how General La Salle found out about the dungeon. Why did he rescue the man?

D. Write the letter of the definition in column II that most closely matches each word in column I.

I. Word	II. Definition
1. heretic	A. loss of hope
2. despair	B. shaped like the moon in its first quarter
3. scythe	C. a church group that punished disbelievers
4. folly	D. bad; nasty
5. dungeon	E. ill feeling arising from distrust or envy of another
6. foul	F. foolishness
7. lured	G. a dark underground prison
8. Inquisition	H. a curved blade fastened to a curved handle; used in mowing hay
9. jealousy	I. one who does not believe in the teachings of his church
10. crescent-shaped	J. tempted

The Secret of
Tilting Rock

Ralph V. Cutlip

I

Tod Enfield paused for a moment of rest in the shade of a small chestnut tree that stood at the edge of the narrow, rocky road. He sensed the rapid beating of his heart, and he licked at the dryness in his mouth. The afternoon air was warm and lazy, and the quietness of the mountain wilderness held him strangely. He was aware of no sound other than his own heavy breathing. As he rested, he became more conscious of the two plowshares[1] he carried, tied together with a loop of wire.

Suddenly below him a flock of crows flapped from the shadows of a beech tree. There had been one cry of alarm, and the crows broke cover noisily and were soon high above the valley in silent flight.

Tod breathed more easily for a moment, and then he heard the clinking steps of horses on the road. The sounds multiplied, and a patrol of Confederate cavalry[2] rounded a

165

bend and began the steep climb toward Snicker's Gap,[3] a half mile farther up the mountainside.

Tod dropped down behind a rock and watched the troopers as they urged their horses up the steep hill. He had seen many horsemen and marching men since the war started, but now before his eyes was action that seemed mighty important. The horses had been ridden hard. Where saddle straps clung to horsehide, there were patches of sweaty foam. The nostrils of each horse were rigid and struggling for air. Several pack horses labored under the weight of their burdens. The troopers were unsmiling and looked serious.

Although Tod was only seventeen, he knew he too was playing an important part in this great drama of war between the states. His family was accused of disloyalty to the South after his father had disappeared from home one day. His mother kept explaining his disappearance to the neighbors by saying, "Father is working up near Winchester. He will be back when the war's over; we got to keep living somehow if one side or t'other don't steal us blind." Tod said nothing; he had been sworn to secrecy.

After the last trooper had ridden by, he lay down in the shade of a clump of laurel. He dozed for a few moments and then came to life, trembling, aroused by a noise in the leaves, less than ten feet away. A large blacksnake ruffled[4] the dry leaves. Tod shuddered as he watched the snake disappear into the end of a hollow log.

He rose to his feet with a bound. He realized how important his errand was, and he hoped he could get through the gap safely. Instead of walking along the road, he slipped through the woodland quietly, going around the dry leaf beds and the rocky slopes. Like a shadow he moved through the forest tunnels with the caution of a hunter, knowing that in a few minutes he might become the hunted if any of the horsemen saw him.

Suddenly he came to an opening in the forest. He could

see the dusty road where it led to the gap, an opening through the mountain range, flanked on each side by rocky slopes that rose steeply for several hundred feet. Tod climbed to the top of a rock for a better look at the gap. His body shook with excitement when he saw that the horsemen had dismounted. Now he could hear the chopping of axes. As he looked, a trooper led a horse from the little roadside creek to the shelter of a beech tree that looked like a huge umbrella in the distance. Across the creek he saw the smooth outline of the top of a field tent. The gap had been secured by a unit of Confederate cavalry. What Tod did not know was that other gaps in the Blue Ridge had been seized by other Confederate cavalry units. The thunderclouds of war were racing to a storm!

Tod climbed down from the rock and picked up the plowshares. He leaned against the rock for a minute, debating with himself what to do. Then he looked down at his left boot. He smiled when he thought of the innersole[5] he had fixed so that it could be pulled back with a hook. Only Tod knew the secret. At that moment a thin piece of folded paper, sealed tightly, lay under the ball of his left foot. Tod knew that somehow he had to get through the gap and leave the message in a hiding place, which was a half mile beyond the top of the gap.

His immediate problem, he knew, was to get past the guards safely. He thought of the little path that led around the hillside above the road; then he realized if he tried to use the path and was caught, he would surely be accused of being a spy. At the same time he knew that if he took the road and was stopped, he would be searched.

Tod came to a quick decision. He stepped boldly into the road and walked toward the gap. As he neared the Confederate camp, he was stopped by a guard who had stepped out from his hiding place behind some bushes.

"Halt! Who goes there?" a bearded trooper commanded.

"Who, me? I . . . I'm Tod Enfield," Tod said. "I'm on my way
to Perry's forge."[6]

"You will have to come to headquarters!" the guard commanded.
"Let's go . . . now!"

The rest of the way was quite
steep, and Tod began to sweat
from heat and worry.

In a few minutes he stood at
the open doorway of a tent. A high-
ranking officer sat on a camp stool
at a small table. He seemed to be
studying a map. He wore the insignia[7] of a brigadier general.

The guard spoke to the order-
ly[8] outside the tent: "Tell the general this boy is trying to get through
the gap."

The orderly turned and spoke
to a lieutenant who sat just inside the doorway.

The lieutenant came outside. "What is it?" he asked.

"This boy says he's on his way to Perry's forge. I stopped
him," the guard replied.

"All right, Blake, you may go," the lieutenant said.

The lieutenant looked at Tod for a moment and then
said, "I guess if you're just going to a shop to get the plow
points sharpened, you won't mind being searched."

Tod felt the fear gripping his body. "Maw says I got
to be back home before dark," he said. His voice was now
pleading.

"Where's your father?" the lieutenant asked.

"I don't know; I guess the Yankees got him."

"Oh, so, he's a prisoner. Well, I am sorry, but we have

to be careful. Before we let you pass through our lines, you'll have to be searched. Off with your clothes!"

Shaking with fear, Tod peeled off his shirt and pants. The lieutenant handed the shirt to a sergeant who had now joined the group. The two men went through the clothing quickly, turning every pocket inside out.

"What's the money for?" the lieutenant asked as he handed it back to Tod.

"Ten cents apiece for sharpening the plow points," Tod answered quietly, surprised by his own calmness.

The lieutenant smiled and took Tod's old felt hat, which he handed to the sergeant. Tod's long, blond hair tumbled over his forehead and his blue eyes flashed, but he said nothing.

"Take off your boots!" the lieutenant commanded.

Trembling, Tod bent forward quickly to hide the expression on his face. He untied the leather laces and handed the boots to the officer, who examined each one in turn. When he picked up the left boot, cold chills gripped Tod. He had a horrible vision of having to face a hanging squad. He felt like weeping when the officer handed his boots back with a quick order: "Get dressed!" Then he disappeared into the tent.

Immediately the general came to the doorway. He hooked his thumbs into his belt and looked at Tod rather sternly but not unkindly.

"What's your name, bub?" he asked.

"Tod Enfield, sir."

The general smiled. "Where do you live?" he asked.

"On the Right Hand Fork, on the old Hampton farm."

"Are you a Virginian?"

Tod nodded and answered quietly, "I was born on the farm."

The general turned to go back inside the tent, then he paused, turned on his heel and said, "You had better be back before dark; you don't want to worry your mother, do you?"

"No, sir!" Tod exclaimed. "Thank you."

II

When Tod was safely out of camp, he began to walk faster but he dared not run. A half mile beyond the gap, on the western side of the ridge, he paused a moment to pick some raspberries. The berries were not fully ripe, but he had time to look along the road in both directions. Satisfied that no one followed, he left the road and hid behind a rock. He remained perfectly quiet for several minutes.

Leaving the roadside, he began to climb the side of the mountain. He moved cautiously from rock to tree and from tree to rock until he had climbed over a hundred feet. He walked around a rock ledge that looked like a huge table and then he hid behind a tree. He could see it now—Tilting Rock, an egg-shaped stone that lay near the middle of the table, weighing more than a thousand pounds. Very few people had ever seen it. Tod and his father had discovered the rock one day when they were squirrel hunting. The rock was a freak of nature. It was so well balanced that a small weight or a little pressure on either end would cause it to teeter[9] gently. Although the giant rock table was well hidden by tall pines and oaks, Tod listened quietly for several minutes before moving.

The time had come! With quick movements he took the looped wire from the plow points and straightened it. One end of the wire had been bent into a small hook. Tod removed his left boot. He pushed the wire into the boot up to the toe. He tried to hook the edge of the innersole where it pressed tightly against the toe. Once . . . twice . . . three times the hook missed. No wonder the lieutenant didn't find the secret hiding place! Tod began to work faster. Back and forth he pushed the wire in rapid strokes. He smiled with satisfaction when he felt the hook catch and pull back the innersole. His quick fingers grabbed the leather tip and pulled it back. In a moment he had the thin piece of paper. Putting his boot back on, he picked up a stick that lay among the rocks and then he climbed boldly onto the table. He raised one end of Tilting Rock and set the stick under it. He knew exactly how to do it, because he had done it many times before. Getting down on his hands and knees, he felt along the underside of Tilting Rock until he found the deep crack he knew about. He slipped the paper into the crack tightly, took the stick away, and let the rock roll back into its former position. Then he climbed down from the table. He knew that within a few hours his father would somehow make his way along the western side of the Blue Ridge, find the message, and then return to the Union lines at Harpers Ferry.

Tod smiled in satisfaction as he hurried on to Perry's forge. He knew that old man Perry could sharpen the plow points in twenty minutes, and he would be back through the gap before dark. He smiled again when he thought how he would show the Confederates his plow points, sharp and gleaming.

III

Now Tod was a curious boy. The events of the great war between the states and his own dangerous missions as a spy had whetted[10] his curiosity, but he did not dare to open the sealed letter and read it. He suspected, of course, that he had become involved in an important military action. There were other spies and scouts moving through the hills and gaps of the Blue Ridge and the broad valley of the Shenandoah.

Perhaps some of them carried the same message as the one Tod left at Tilting Rock.

The letter that Tod left for his father was unsigned except for a crudely drawn picture of an ear of corn. The wording was as follows:

> Richmond, Virginia, May 10, 1863. Lee's army to invade the North by way of Shenandoah Valley and the Cumberland Valley.
>
> The First, Second, and Third Corps of the Confederate Army of Northern Virginia will move out from Fredericksburg about June 3d.
>
> Lee's plan is to take Harrisburg and threaten Washington. Stuart's cavalry will lead the way. Imboden and Jenkins will occupy all the Blue Ridge gaps to secure the safety of the army.

Tod naturally felt great pride in his service to the Union. But he did not know that on the afternoon of his great adventure he had stood face to face with Brigadier John D. Imboden, who had kindly let him pass on his way to Tilting Rock.

• *Building Your Vocabulary*

1.	**plowshares**	sharp points for a plow
2.	**cavalry**	soldiers on horseback
3.	**gap**	an opening; a mountain pass
4.	**ruffled**	disturbed; mussed
5.	**innersole**	a loose, thin strip placed inside a shoe usually for warmth or comfort
6.	**forge**	a shop with a furnace to heat and shape metal
7.	**insignia**	a badge or emblem of rank
8.	**orderly**	a soldier who assists an officer
9.	**teeter**	to seesaw; to waver up and down
10.	**whetted**	sharpened; increased

● *Exercises*

A. Write the letter of the expression that best completes each of the following statements:

1. Tod Enfield's age was _____.
   a. eighteen   *b*. seventeen   *c*. sixteen

2. Tod shuddered as he watched the snake disappear into _____.
   a. a hole in a tree
   b. a hole in the ground
   c. the end of a hollow log

3. Tod climbed to the top of a rock for a better look at _____.
   a. the soldiers' camp
   b. the gap
   c. the valley

4. Only Tod knew the secret of _____.
   a. the innersole of his boot
   b. where his father was
   c. Snicker's Gap

5. The message Tod carried was unsigned except for a crudely drawn sketch of _____.
   a. a cornstalk   *b*. an ear of corn   *c*. an acorn

B. Decide whether each of the following statements is true or false. Write T for *true* and F for *false*.

1. Tod carried three plowshares, tied together with a loop of wire.

2. After the last trooper had ridden by, Tod lay down in the shade of a clump of laurel.

3. Snicker's Gap had been secured by a unit of Yankee cavalry.

4. Tod realized that if he took the road and was stopped, he would be searched.

5. Tod said he was on his way to a mill.

6. The lieutenant found some money in Tod's clothes.
7. Very few people had ever seen Tilting Rock.
8. Tod carried a secret message under the innersole of his right boot.
9. Tod knew the contents of the message.
10. The Confederate officers allowed Tod to continue his way through Snicker's Gap.

C. Write the letter of the definition in column II that most closely matches each word in column I.

I. Word	II. Definition
1. cavalry	A. a soldier who assists an officer
2. whetted	B. disturbed; mussed
3. ruffled	C. to seesaw; to waver up and down
4. insignia	D. an opening; a mountain pass
5. orderly	E. soldiers on horseback
6. innersole	F. sharpened; increased
7. teeter	G. sharp points for a plow
8. gap	H. a badge or emblem of rank
9. forge	I. a loose, thin strip placed inside a shoe usually for warmth or comfort
10. plowshares	J. a shop with a furnace to heat and shape metal

D. Write one or two paragraphs on one of the following topics:
1. Tell about Tod's adventures up to the moment he was stopped by the guard.
2. Tell what happened to Tod in the Confederate camp.
3. After Tod was released, what did he do?
4. Imagine that a Confederate trooper was ordered to follow Tod. Tell what happened.